CONTENTS

ABOUT THE AUTHOR

George Wuerthner is a full-time free-lance photographer, writer, and ecologist. He has written thirteen other titles including *Yellowstone—A Visitor's Companion, Alaska Mountain Ranges, Forever Wild—The Adirondacks, Big Bend Country, Southern Appalachian Country, Montana—Magnificent Wilderness, Idaho Mountain Ranges, Nevada Mountain Ranges, Oregon Mountain Ranges,* and *The Maine Coast.* In addition, his photos have appeared in hundreds of calendars, books, magazines, and other publications. He has also exhibited at the Smithsonian Institution and other museums.

Wuerthner graduated from the University of Montana with degrees in wildlife biology and botany and received a master's degree in science communication from the University of California, Santa Cruz. A former wilderness ranger, national park ranger, botanist, science teacher, university instructor, and guide, Wuerthner now lives in Livingston, Montana, north of Yellowstone National Park.

Yosemite

YOSEMITE

A Visitor's Companion

George Wuerthner

Photographs by George Wuerthner

STACKPOLE
BOOKS

Published by
STACKPOLE BOOKS
5067 Ritter Road
Mechanicsburg, PA 17055

Printed in the United States of America

10 9 8 7 6 5 4 3

First Edition
Cover design by Mark Olszewski
Thanks to Ruthie Matteson for her help with the illustrations.

To Mollie Matteson, my wife. Yosemite is where we went on our first date.

Library of Congress Cataloging-in-Publication Data

Wuerthner, George.
    Yosemite : a visitor's companion / George Wuerthner.
        p.   cm.
    Includes index.
    ISBN 0-8117-2598-7
    1. Natural history—California—Yosemite National Park—
Guidebooks.   2. Yosemite National Park (Calif.)—Guidebooks.
I. Title.
QH105.C2W83   1994
508.794'47—dc20   93-41463
                                                                          CIP

ACKNOWLEDGMENTS

Many people assisted me in the researching of this book. The following folks helped me in some way: Scott Carpenter, Sallie Hejl, Stephen Sackett, Albert Parker, John Helms, Stanford Demars, Jeffrey Keay, Jan Van Wagtendonk, Peter Koehler, David Peterson, Thomas Vale, Laura Munsen, Jeffrey Schaffer, Gordon Gould, Jim Eaton, and Ginger Burley. Many Park Service people answered questions for me and in many cases I did not get their names; however, I thank all of them. Finally, thanks to John Muir for advocating Yosemite's protection a hundred years ago; without him, we would not have the park to argue about today. And thanks to the people who have continued to work for a better Yosemite since then, including many individuals in the Park Service, Sierra Club, Wilderness Society, California Wilderness Coalition, and other organizations.

Special thanks to Ruthie Matteson for producing some of the line art used in this guide.

Introduction

California's Sierra Nevada is one of the most spectacular mountain uplifts within the United States. More than four hundred miles end to end, it ranks as the longest continuous mountain range in the United States. The Rockies, Appalachians, and Cascades are longer but broken up into numerous subranges. On its eastern flank, the Sierra rises more than two miles above the Owens Valley, nearly double the elevational rise of the Tetons. Lake Tahoe—more than half a mile in depth—is the second deepest lake in the United States, and the tenth deepest in the world. The Sierran woodlands are considered by many to be the finest coniferous forests found anywhere and the giant sequoia, one of the most magnificent tree species on earth. Yet in this range of superlatives, there is no place where more of its many celebrated attributes are found than Yosemite National Park.

Here are four of the ten highest waterfalls in the world, including 2,425-foot Yosemite Falls (really a series of falls and cascades). The granite face of El Capitan is one of the sheerest and highest on earth. The rounded summit of 8,842-foot Half Dome rises 4,754 feet above Mirror Lake at its base; it is one of the most extraordinary and photographed mountains anywhere. Tuolumne Meadows is the largest subalpine meadow in the entire Sierra. Tamarack Flat along the Tioga Pass road is the geographic center of the Sierra. It is two hundred miles north or south to either end of the range from here. And there is no more striking valley in all of the range, and perhaps the entire West, than the Yosemite.

For these reasons and more, Yosemite was also the first wild land protected by Congress. In 1864, eight years before Yellowstone was set aside as a national park, Congress deeded land to the state of California in order to protect the Yosemite Valley as a state park. The early recognition of Yosemite's extraordinary scenic qualities is certainly one of the chief reasons this portion of the central Sierra was given national park status

1

The rounded summit of Half Dome, shown here as seen from Washburn Point, is a favorite of photographers.

in 1890; this made the Yosemite region our third national park, after Sequoia and Yellowstone. More recently, in 1984 the United Nations recognized its world-class values by proclaiming Yosemite a World Heritage Site. It would be difficult to argue with the authors of Yosemite's master plan, who conclude that the valley is "one of the grandest natural settings that exist anywhere in the world."

Today more than 3.5 million visitors (78 percent from California) drive, stroll, hike, ski, and some would even suggest "swarm," over the park's twelve hundred square miles, all vying for the park's several thousand campsites and backcountry permits. Smoke and noise have replaced much of the original peace that drew people like conservationist John Muir to Yosemite in the first place. Yet, as with all popular recreational areas, most of the use is concentrated in a small fraction of the landscape, with an estimated 70 percent of the visitation occurring in the seven-mile-long Yosemite Valley.

During the summer months, the valley becomes a mini-city with as many as 20,000 people a day jamming the parking lots, campgrounds, and hiking trails. To take care of this number of people, the Park Service has 385 full- and part-time employees, plus as many as 370 seasonal workers. The concessionaires hire another 1,800 summer workers. Housing and catering to the needs of this mass of humanity have resulted in the construction of hotels, restaurants, tent camps, even ice rinks and golf courses, which some suggest degrades the scenic and spiritual qualities of the valley. A heated debate about which park and concession facilities are necessary and which could or should be removed from the park has dragged on for decades. It seems no closer to resolution than it was a hundred years ago when the first concerns about overdevelopment were initially expressed.

Despite the carnival atmosphere in the valley, anyone taking the time to move beyond the few popular destinations and overlooks can still find the tranquility and beauty that drew Yosemite's most famous resident, John Muir, to the mountains more than a hundred years ago. Like the granite walls that enclose the valley, the passage of time and human efforts to "improve" upon nature have left their mark but have not destroyed Yosemite. The park endures and continues to inspire visitors with its grandeur.

Geographic Setting

Yosemite National Park is just one of more than four hundred units managed by the National Park Service. The park protects some 748,542 acres of the central Sierra Nevada, or an area about the size of Rhode Island. Only one highway, the Tioga Pass road, bisects the park, more or less dividing it into two equal halves. Mining, livestock grazing, hunting, logging, and unregulated ORV use are typically not permitted in national parks, although there are some exceptions. National parks are usually managed to maintain their ecological, historic, geologic, spiritual, scenic, and recreational values.

Yosemite is surrounded by other federal lands. These are primarily administrated by the Forest Service with a smaller amount under the care of the Bureau of Land Management. To the west and north is the Stanislaus National Forest, to the southwest, the Sierra National Forest, and bordering the park's eastern flank are the Inyo and Toyiabe National Forests. Unlike the National Park Service, the Forest Service operates under a "multiple use" concept. Ideally, this means many different activities, including extractive industries—such as logging, mining, and grazing—along with recreation and biodiversity preservation, are all permitted without severely compromising each other. In reality, this seldom happens, and many heated debates have ensued over what constitutes the "best" use of these lands.

Fortunately, for Yosemite visitors as well as the park's biological integrity, most Forest Service lands immediately surrounding the park are managed primarily as wilderness, a land classification that does not permit logging, mining, or the use of motorized vehicles. The one exception to an otherwise ideal preservation system is the clause that permits grazing domestic livestock in wilderness. Of all the human activities that influence the Sierra Nevada, none has probably done more biological harm. Fortunately, on most Forest Service land immediately adjacent to Yosemite, livestock use is nearly non-existent.

Additional protection to adjacent Forest Service land is offered by the Mono Lake National Scenic Area administered by the Inyo National Forest. The Scenic Area lies east of Yosemite and is accessible by the Tioga Pass road. The recent construction of visitor centers in Lee Vining and in Mammoth Lakes represents an increased emphasis by the Forest Service on interpretation and recreational enhancement rather than extractive uses.

Lying south and east of San Francisco and major Central Valley population centers such as Sacramento, Yosemite is within a day's drive of thirty million people. Yet, immediately adjacent to the park, there are few large population centers. On the west slope are Oakhurst, Mariposa, El Portal, and Big Oak Flat, none of which has more than a few thousand inhabitants. Lee Vining and Bridgeport, small communities nestled at the base of the peaks on the eastern slope, have no more than a few hundred souls each. The winding roads leading to Yosemite climb and fall as they trace the margins of ridges and dive into deep river canyons. Furthermore, Yosemite is not on the road to anywhere. You don't drive through the park on your way to Sacramento, Reno, or Los Angeles. You have to make a conscious decision to visit the place. Distance from major urban centers and lack of access are, perhaps more than any other factors, responsible for Yosemite's protection and keep it from being completely overrun.

The Sierra Nevada range lies between the Central Valley on the west and the Great Basin on the east. The Central Valley is a nearly level plain almost entirely surrounded by mountains. From twenty-five to seventy miles across and running more than four hundred miles north and south, the valley is drained by two major rivers, the Sacramento and the San Joaquin. The two major rivers in Yosemite—the Merced and the Tuolumne—are both tributaries of the San Joaquin. At one time the Central Valley was home to vast herds of pronghorn antelope and Tule elk along with grizzlies and skeins of ducks and geese. Today the valley has been converted to agricultural fields and urban centers such as Stockton, Sacramento, Fresno, and Bakersfield.

East of the Sierra lies the Great Basin Province, a seven-hundred-mile-wide swath of fault block mountain ranges separated by wide, desert basins. Sagebrush dominates the valleys; forests of pinyon pine, aspen, and juniper cloak many of the mountain slopes.

Ranging from 2,000 feet along the Merced River to more than 13,114 feet on the summit of Mount Lyell, Yosemite encompasses nearly all life zones found in the Sierra Nevada range except for the low-elevation grasslands.

The Sierra Nevada is a fault block mountain uplift. Its long western flank is a gentle ramp of mostly granitic bedrock rising steadily from the Central Valley to a high point near the eastern margin; from there it falls sharply toward the fault that marks its border. The westward tilt of the range is obvious to anyone who climbs one of the park's higher peaks.

Along the eastern edge of the park lie most of the higher peaks with many exceeding 12,000 feet. Since one of the reasons for establishing Yosemite National Park was to protect the watersheds of the Merced and Tuolumne rivers, it's not surprising that the watershed divide along the crest of the range marks the park's eastern boundary.

Beginning ten million years ago the Sierran block was pushed up and tilted, increasing the gradient of its streams. The resulting turbulent streams, and later glacial ice, have carved canyons through which rivers

Glaciers have steepened the flanks of this ridge above Nelson Lake in the Cathedral Range.

like the Merced and Tuolumne descend as much as four thousand feet into the western flank of the range. As a consequence, travel north and south across the grain of the range is difficult, requiring steep descents into canyons, and equally steep climbs back out. To avoid these descents and ascents, most of the roads outside the Yosemite Valley follow the ridges between river canyons. The eastern flank of the range, though it has steeper gradients, nevertheless has much smaller watershed basins from which to collect water; hence, it tends to have modest, short canyons.

Because of the elevational gradient, a tremendous diversity of plants grows within the park. Botanists estimate that a minimum of fourteen hundred species occur in the park including thirty-seven tree species, eighteen of them conifers.

The lowest, driest slopes are covered mostly with brushy chaparral and oak savanna, which gradually grades into pine forest at about the 4,000-foot level. In the middle elevations between 6,000 and 8,000 feet lies the band of heaviest precipitation and greatest forest cover. This is where the magnificent forests of red fir, giant sequoia, and sugar pine are found. Around 8,000 feet to 10,000 or more feet one finds the subalpine zone of lodgepole forest intermixed with other species like mountain hemlock and whitebark pine. Meadows are abundant in this zone, as is bare rock. Here, also, are most of the park's more than three hundred lakes, scoured from bedrock by glaciers that in some cases only retreated a century ago. At the highest elevations are alpine tundra and rock. The Yosemite alpine zone, although not as extensive as farther south in the range, is still a significant part of the park's natural features.

The diversity of habitats supports a wide variety of animals. There are 6 native fish species, plus 5 introduced species, including brook trout. Twenty-nine species of amphibians and reptiles call Yosemite home, along with more than 240 species of birds and 77 species of mammals.

Despite the many people who live within driving distance of the park, a large percentage of the park and the surrounding federal land is maintained in a natural condition. Although obvious enough on a map, on the ground the boundaries between the park and adjacent federal lands are blurred, in part because much of the surrounding land is managed as wilderness, which prohibits roads, motorized vehicles, and most kinds of resource extraction—in other words essentially the same kind of management emphasis one finds in national parks. Even within Yosemite National Park, more than 94 percent of the park (706,348 acres) is managed as designated wilderness that cannot be developed.

CLIMATE

Compared with nearly every other major mountain range in the United States, the climate of the Sierra Nevada is relatively benign. This is one reason why some have dubbed the range "Gentle Wilderness." Below-zero temperatures are unusual. Summers are nearly rainless; only 3 percent of the annual precipitation occurs in this season.

Generalizations about Yosemite's weather must be considered within the context of elevation. When spring flowers are blooming in March along the lower Merced River, it may be snowing and well below freezing near the headwaters along the slopes of Mount Lyell. Nevertheless, there are some common patterns that apply to the entire park.

There are two major influences upon Yosemite's climate. One is the close proximity of the Pacific Ocean; the other is the Sierra Nevada mountains themselves. The ocean affects the weather in several ways. Less than a hundred miles from the moderating maritime influence of the sea, the Sierra Nevada experiences fewer temperature extremes than say the Rockies with their more continental climate.

California in general, and Yosemite in particular, experiences what is called a Mediterranean climate, which is characterized by a wet and a dry season such as one might encounter in Italy or Greece. In California, winters are normally wet. During this season, Pacific storm tracks shift southward, bringing rain to much of California and snow to the high country. In the Yosemite high country, snow typically doesn't stay on the ground until sometime in November and then accumulates all winter, reaching its greatest depth in late March or early April. Yet, despite the snow, on many winter days the temperatures in Yosemite Valley may reach up into the forties and fifties, in part because of the moderating maritime influence.

In summer, the storm tracks shift northward, and a Pacific anticyclone air mass docks itself off the California coast. This creates a cool, onshore flow of marine air that results in fog in places like San Francisco but clear, dry air in the Sierra.

Elevation and Orographic Lift

Just as the ocean influences climatic conditions, the Sierra Nevada modifies weather as well. The range acts as a barrier to the movement of moisture-laden air coming off the Pacific and helps to protect the west slope and the rest of California from the cold arctic air masses that occasionally invade the Great Basin. Also, because of its great height, it markedly changes the climate, creating local weather patterns. For each thousand-foot rise, air pressure decreases, with a corresponding temperature drop of three and a half degrees. Thus while Sacramento may be sweltering in one-hundred-degree temperatures, it may be a moderate seventy-five degrees at 9,945-foot Tioga Pass, the eastern entrance to Yosemite.

During the winter months, the Pacific Ocean continuously spawns cyclonic storms that sweep moist, relatively warm air inland. As these air masses encounter the Sierran wall and begin to ascend its long western slope, they cool; this reduces their capacity to hold water. The water vapor condenses into clouds and frequently falls to the ground as rain or snow. Because the western slope is so long and the mountain barrier so high, air masses tend to stall as they attempt to climb over the range. As a result, most of the moisture within a cloud falls before the air mass clears the top of the range. Consequently, the eastern flank of the Sierra is in the rain shadow of the western slope and receives little moisture. This is one reason why the Great Basin desert begins immediately to the east of the Sierra Nevada.

In the summer, daytime heating of air over the Central Valley causes it to rise and cool. As these rising air masses sweep eastward and upward over the mountains, battalions of puffy, white cumulus clouds suddenly sprout in the afternoon sky. These sometimes result in thunder showers; more often they merely spawn some sound and fury but little rain. By evening, after the air cools down, the clouds disappear, and the sky clears to another star-filled night.

Once these air masses clear the tops of the Sierran crest, they sweep down the eastern flank. As they do so they become warmer, thus increasing their ability to hold moisture. These descending air masses actually dry the landscape they pass over, sucking up available moisture. They are another reason the eastern side of the Sierra is so arid.

Weather Through the Year

A typical January day in Yosemite Valley is likely to be cloudy; the weather is sunny only 39 percent of the time. Nearly seven inches of precipitation will fall during the month. As much as 90 percent of the annual precipitation comes during the months of November, December, January, February, and March. At elevations below 2,000 feet nearly all precipitation typically falls as rain, but above 6,000 feet snow is the rule.

In a representative year, snow depth at 4,000 feet in the Yosemite Valley does not exceed two feet. However, the high country can and does receive far more snow, and depths may exceed fifteen feet or more. Annual snowfall totals thirty-five to forty inches in the valley, but fifty to sixty inches or more are common at higher elevations. The greatest snowfall occurs from 6,000 to 8,000 feet. Above this elevation, annual precipitation actually drops slightly.

The Spanish name Sierra Nevada means snowy mountain range, and certainly the Sierra earns this title. This is one of the snowiest parts of the United States, exceeded only by mountains in Alaska and the Pacific Northwest. A little north of Yosemite, at Tamarack, California, the North American record for snowfall in a single month was set in January 1911 when thirty-two and a half feet fell! And snowfall of up to forty feet in a single winter has been recorded at Mammoth Mountain slightly south of Yosemite.

Occasionally, cold arctic fronts from Canada sweep down into the Great Basin, bringing temperatures as low as twenty-five degrees below zero to some of the valleys along the eastern slope of the Sierra. However, such extreme temperatures are almost never experienced in Yosemite, in part because of its location on the western slope of the range.

In summer, the offshore high pressure air mass remains stationary, preventing the formation of rain clouds. Typically, summers in Yosemite are nearly rainless, except for an occasional thunderstorm. In contrast to the 39 percent sunshine of January, in July the sun shines approximately 97 percent of the time. Precipitation drops to less than half an inch for the entire month. August is even drier, with an average of six hundredths of an inch of precipitation! No wonder many backpackers don't even bother with carrying a tent during the summer months in Yosemite.

Most summer days in Yosemite are very comfortable. Low humidity tempers any heat, making it bearable if not ideal. The low humidity means the air can hold little heat, and rapid nighttime cooling is the norm. Even after the warmest days, the nights are nearly always cool and sometimes even cold. I have experienced below-freezing temperatures above 10,000 feet in July. Even after days when it was comfortable to wear nothing more than shorts and a T-shirt, it may be necessary to put on a down jacket and a hat at night.

Intense solar radiation results from the nearly cloudless skies. This combined with the continuous summer drought makes the Sierra Nevada's alpine vegetation more depauperate than that of other major mountain ranges such as the Rockies or even the Cascades.

The summer drought that characterizes California is so pronounced that if it were not for the winter snowpack held by the Sierra, most of California would be uninhabitable desert. The slow melting of snow well into the middle of summer provides the moisture that fills reservoirs and irrigation canals in the Central Valley and beyond. Likewise, most plant growth is dependent upon winter moisture reserves in the soil or from snowmelt.

Autumn is often considered the best time of year to visit Yosemite, in part because most of the crowds are gone, but also because of the good weather. The days are warm and nearly always sunny, and the nights are cool but seldom frigid, except at the highest elevations.

HISTORY

The history of Yosemite Park and the Sierra Nevada has, in many ways, mirrored changing attitudes of Americans toward the landscape and its people. The first Europeans sought to extract riches from furs, gold, and timber. They destroyed native Indian cultures and society and rapaciously abused natural resources; however, the Sierra Nevada was also the focus of some of the earliest conservation efforts. Yosemite Valley was protected as a state park in 1864; this was one of the earliest efforts to preserve scenic values in the nation. The Sierra National Forest, which surrounds parts of Yosemite, was established in 1891 as one of the first forest reserves in the country. And it was here that conservationists from John Muir to David Brower got their inspiration to fight for the preservation of Yosemite as well as many other parts of the earth. Thus the history of Yosemite is in many ways a microcosm of the history of the West.

Early Inhabitants

The written history of Yosemite begins with the first expansion of the fur trappers into the far West, but prior to their explorations California, including the Yosemite area, was already home to diverse peoples. Some were relatively recent immigrants to California, who arrived in the state at the same time as or slightly before Europeans. The Monache, a Shoshonean-speaking group, occupied the southern Sierra only within the past three to five hundred years, coming from the deserts to the east. Other groups may trace their ancestors back to the original human occupants of this region.

Although people have been in California since the closing of the last Ice Age, evidence for human occupation of Yosemite dates only from the past three thousand years. By this time, the vegetation and wildlife of the region closely resembled what is there today. Acorns, deer, salmon, and other food resources were abundant on the western slope of the Sierra

Nevada, while pinyon nuts and obsidian for arrowheads were found on the eastern side of the mountains. Seeking these resources, people traveled back and forth on trading and raiding expeditions.

Archaeologists recognize three cultural phases among these groups. The earliest, the Crane Flat Phase, dates from 1000 B.C. to 500 A.D. People of this period relied upon hunting with the atl atl, a shaft that permitted a short spear to be thrown. They also used grinding stones; this suggests that they ate seeds.

The next identified phase, the Tarmarack, began about 500 A.D. and lasted until 1200 A.D., or about the time that Greenland was abandoned by the Vikings. A shift to smaller rock points indicates the adoption of the bow and arrow. The bow permitted more efficient hunting of wildlife. Acorns were added to the diet.

The final phase, the Mariposa, began at 1200 A.D. and continued up until Euroamerican contact. The diet continued to improve and become more varied. Hunting and gathering were still the major sources of food, but trading with other tribes became more widespread. Clam shells in archaeological sites indicate some contact with coastal people. Historians have calculated that at the time of the first European settlement of California, an estimated 133,000 Indians—one of the densest pre-European populations in North America—resided in what would eventually become the Golden State.

Exploration

Though only two hundred miles from the coast, Yosemite Valley remained unknown to Euroamericans for decades, despite a century of Spanish settlement in California. The Spanish did not operate any missions or settlements more than twenty-five miles from the coast. Although they named the Sierra, they did not visit it.

It was not until 1827 that the first Euroamericans penetrated the Sierra. The American fur trapper Jedediah Smith led a band of trappers from Wyoming into southern California. After being rebuked by the Spanish authorities there, Smith turned north and went into the Central Valley, where he followed the Sierra Nevada searching for beaver as well as a place to cross the range. In May 1827 Smith and two companions (he left the other trappers in the Central Valley) succeeded in crossing the Sierra by Ebbetts Pass north of Yosemite. This was the first successful crossing of the Sierra by white people.

Returning to the Rockies, Smith recounted his adventures in sunny

California to other trappers. Soon other adventurers sought trails to the west coast. One of these, Joseph Walker, led a party of trappers across Nevada in 1833. Following his namesake, the Walker River, into the mountains, he encountered the east side of the Sierra Nevada somewhere near present-day Bridgeport. It was late October. Snow in the higher elevations made it difficult to traverse the range. Walker's party lost many of their horses as they floundered in the deep snow.

As they wandered along the ridges, they eventually came to a place that Zenas Leonard, one of Walker's men, described in his journal. They saw many small streams drop " . . . themselves from one lofty precipice to another, until they are exhausted in rain below. Some of these precipices appeared to us to be more than a mile high." The only place where such waterfalls and cliffs exist is Yosemite. This would make Walker's party the first Euroamericans to see the Yosemite Valley, although they did not enter it.

Two days later Leonard noted in his journal that the party encountered some trees "of the redwood species, incredibly large—some of which would measure from 16 to 18 fathoms round the trunk at the height of a man's head from the ground." Undoubtedly they stumbled upon the Tuolumne or Merced sequoia groves, and became the first whites to note these giant forests of the Sierra. But Leonard's journals were not published until years later. In the great expanse of the western United States, with its widespread scenic grandeur, neither the hidden Yosemite Valley nor the giant sequoia trees discovered by the Walker party warranted special note. It remained for future visitors to bring the valley's marvels to the attention of the world.

Contact

The first white contact with Indians living in the Yosemite area came immediately after the discovery of gold in 1848, when Euroamericans flooded into the Sierra foothills seeking the valuable metal. At this time, indigenous people lived on both sides of the Sierra except for the highest elevations. Within Yosemite, a subtribe of the Miwok Indians made their homes along the lower elevations of the major river valleys, such as the Merced and Tuolumne. The Miwok spoke a dialect of the Penutian tongue, which was the dominant language among Californian tribes. On occasion Monos, Shoshonean-speaking people from the east side of the

These holes in rocks were used by Sierran Indian tribes to grind up one of their major foods—acorns. Bark huts provided shelter from storms.

Sierra near their namesake, Mono Lake, also visited the Yosemite Valley to trade.

Indians on both sides of the mountains followed a similar seasonal pattern, although they exploited different resources. They moved to lower elevations in winter and to the cooler, forested areas at higher elevations for the summer months, following the upslope movements of deer and other game into the mountains.

These indigenous hunters killed deer with bows and arrows or by communal drives. They went into dens after bears, and smoked smaller mammals like ground squirrels from their burrows to capture them. Even grasshoppers were an important food resource; these too were typically captured in communal drives.

Native inhabitants of Yosemite also speared, netted, or poisoned fish. They crushed buckeye nuts and threw large quantities into streams during the low water of late summer or early fall. When poisoned fish floated to the surface, these were picked up at will.

Although deer and other game contributed to their diets, the staple food of people living on the western slope was acorns. Because acorns could be stored, they acted as a hedge against food shortages. Acorns were soaked and rinsed in water to leach out the tannin, then ground up and cooked to make a mush or paste that could be eaten cold or baked into cakes.

Other foods that were gathered included berries such as chokeberry, serviceberry, and thimbleberry; the latter were usually eaten raw. Manzanita berries were made into a drink. Bulbs, roots, and greens were eaten raw as well as cooked.

On the eastern slope of the mountains, pinyon nuts filled the same purpose as acorns, although the nuts were typically eaten raw. The Monos also gathered brine flies along the shore of Mono Lake. These tiny insects provided a ready source of protein in the summer. In addition to deer, groups living east of the Sierra hunted jackrabbits and pronghorn antelope. The jackrabbits were often caught during communal drives.

People on the east and west sides of the mountains traded with each other. Monos exchanged obsidian, which was used for arrowheads, as well as pinyon nuts, rabbit-skin blankets, salt, and even buffalo robes they obtained from tribes farther east, for acorns and shells supplied by coastal tribes. Some of the trails we still follow today in Yosemite are merely upgraded versions of old Indian trails. For instance, a major trading trail went up the Dana Fork to Mono Pass and down Bloody Canyon to Mono Lake.

Villages were generally located in forests on the edges of meadows. Some were inhabited throughout the year, but others were seasonally occupied. Because of the mild climate and the villagers' semi-mobile lifestyle, most native houses consisted of easily constructed, dome-like brush or bark wickiups; however, partially sunken earthen and wood houses that were approximately forty feet in diameter and resembled hogans from the Southwest were also constructed for ceremonial purposes. Entry was gained by a hole in the roof. One of the larger settlements in the park occupied three-fourths of a mile of the valley floor below Yosemite Falls, near the site of the present Yosemite Village.

The traditional ways of Yosemite's people were relatively unaffected by the coming of the Spanish to California. Except for a few exploratory forays along the base of the Sierra, these Europeans had no contact with inland peoples, although there is evidence that diseases from the Europeans preceded actual contact, often with devastating results. All that changed with the 1848 discovery of gold in California, however. Thousands of gold seekers descended upon the Sierran foothills, and before long their searches took them higher into the mountains. Within one year an estimated one hundred thousand new residents came to California. The immigrants nearly equaled the entire Indian population at the time of Spanish settlement. The miners often displaced indigenous people from their traditional foraging and hunting areas. As if starvation were not enough, the newcomers also carried diseases to which native people had little resistance. Furthermore, many miners shot Indians on sight. Extermination was a government approved policy.

Mariposa Wars

By 1849 the mining camp that would later be known as Big Oak Flat had sprung up along tributaries of the Tuolumne River west of Yosemite. By 1850 there was a trading post and mining operation run by James Savage on the Merced River ten miles west of present-day Yosemite and a similar operation near Mariposa. In December 1850 Indians raided both trading posts and then retreated into the mountains to avoid retribution. The Mariposa Indian Wars had begun.

James Savage organized a punitive party of miners with himself as its scout. In January 1851 Savage attacked a group of Indians. The latter

Tenaya Lake, one of the largest natural lakes in the park, is named for the chief of the Ahwahneeches.

managed to rout Savage's volunteer force. The miners returned to the Central Valley for reinforcements.

In February the Mariposa Battalion was organized with Savage as its leader, and in early March it rode back into the Sierra to seek out the Indian resisters. On the South Fork of the Merced near present-day Wawona, the battalion surprised one Indian group in a pre-dawn raid. The group surrendered without a fight.

Runners were sent out to other Indian villages telling the inhabitants to come in and surrender or suffer the consequences. Some of the people of Yosemite, a subgroup of Miwok known as the Ahwahneeches, along with their chief, Tenaya, surrendered to Savage and his troops; however, many of the Ahwahneeches refused to give themselves up and fled farther into the mountains. Savage, with his troops, set out to capture the rene-gades. They followed their trail to Inspiration Point, where the entire Yosemite Valley was spread out before them with wisps of clouds hanging upon the peaks. Some of the troops recognized that they were seeing something beyond the ordinary. But the task at hand was to capture Indians, so the troops lingered only a moment before they made their way into Yosemite Valley.

They found only one old Indian woman in the valley. It was clear that the rest of the tribe had escaped. Their hastily vacated camps were still scattered throughout the magnificent canyon. To starve the remaining people into submission, Savage burned their acorn granaries and huts. Gathering up Tenaya and his followers, Savage and his troops started back to their base camp in the Central Valley. During the journey, all but one of the Indians escaped and returned to the mountains.

Another military troop was dispatched. Although the soldiers found recent evidence of occupation in Yosemite Valley, the Indians had climbed into the rocky cliffs above the valley floor. From there they watched the troops below. Several Indians were captured, including two of Tenaya's sons. One was later wantonly shot, supposedly trying to escape. Later that day, Tenaya himself was captured.

Following an Indian trail out of the valley, the troops discovered the main body of Tenaya's band camping along the banks of a blue mountain lake, now known as Tenaya. Taken by surprise and suffering from starvation, the Indians were easily captured. Tenaya and what remained of his band were marched to a reservation in the Central Valley. They found the food and heat of the Central Valley unacceptable and were eventually permitted to go back to their mountain home.

The following year, 1852, eight miners from the foothills entered Yosemite Valley. It is unclear what happened next. Some say the miners killed an Indian child; another version of the story suggests that one of the miners wanted several of his partners killed so he could take possession of the jointly owned mine. Whatever the motivation, several of the miners were murdered, and the others immediately retreated from the valley. When the remaining members of the party got to the safety of the settlements, a new punitive Army expedition was dispatched to bring the Indians under control.

Five Indians were captured in the valley. They explained that the miners had been trespassing and had no right to be in the valley. The Army commander claimed that the Indians had signed a treaty giving up their rights to the valley; thus they no longer owned it. The Indians denied they had ever signed away their lands. Regardless of whether Chief Tenaya had signed such a treaty or not, the U.S. Senate subsequently rejected nineteen Indian treaties including the one supposedly signed by the Ahwahneeches. The land was legally still theirs; however, that did the captives little good. They were executed that day. Fearing similar retribution, the rest of the tribe made the journey across the Sierran passes to join the Monos east of the mountains, where they were not pursued. The next year, Chief Tenaya, the last chief of the Ahwahneeches, was stoned to death as a result of a dispute with the Monos. Although Miwok Indians continued to dwell in Yosemite Valley until the 1900s, what remained of the Ahwahneeches scattered. They were never again together as a distinct group.

And so the first Euroamerican contact with Yosemite was one of despoliation and violence. It was not motivated by reverence or even admiration for the landscape's beauty; yet, the splendor of the homeland of the Ahwahneeches was not lost on everyone. The reports of a magnificent valley hidden in the Sierra would soon change the course of history.

Publicity and Settlement

Although it's possible that a few miners or hunters may have entered Yosemite in the years immediately after the California gold rush in 1848, credit for publicizing the place goes to members of the Savage military expedition. Among the troops was a medical doctor, Lafayette Bunnell. Bunnell kept a diary of the expedition and eloquently described the valley's attributes. When he first viewed the entire valley from Old Inspiration Point, Bunnell wrote: "The grandeur of the scene was softened by the haze that hung over the valley—light as gossamer—and by the clouds which partially dimmed the higher cliffs and mountains. This obscurity of vision but increased the awe with which I beheld it, and as I looked, a peculiar exalted sensation seemed to fill my whole being, and I found my eyes in tears wtih emotions." That night around a campfire, Bunnell suggested to his companions that the valley be named for its native people—the "Yosemity." It turns out that this was not their name, but the appellation stuck.

Yosemite might have remained obscure except for James Mason Hutchings, a writer living in San Francisco. Hutchings heard reports of a thousand-foot waterfall in the Sierra. More than five times the height of Niagara, this seemed worthy of investigation. So in June 1855, Hutchings, along with the artist Thomas Ayres and two others, set out for the Sierra. They located a few old Ahwahneeches who offered to guide the

Vernal Falls cascades over a lip of granite along the Mist Trail. The falls was named in 1851 by Lafayette Bunnell, a medical doctor who entered the valley with the Mariposa Battalion.

party to the valley. Upon reaching Old Inspiration Point, the party stopped, and Ayres immediately got out his art supplies to sketch a picture. The group spent five days exploring the valley. Hutchings wrote an account of his trip for a local paper. It was republished nationally, and this drew additional attention to Yosemite. The next year, he began publishing *Hutchings California Magazine*, which promoted the state's features and scenery, including Yosemite.

Word of Yosemite's spectacular falls and cliffs prompted additional exploration that year by local residents. Two other groups visited the valley that summer and rediscovered Vernal and Nevada falls. Previously seen by the members of the Mariposa Battalion, these had since been forgotten. In those days, such journeys were unusual. Here were people traveling at great effort to a distant valley not to mine its mountains for ore or to shoot its wildlife, but merely to view its scenic wonders.

Forty-eight people visited Yosemite in 1855. This trickle soon became a flood, as word of the area's magnificence spread beyond the local settlements. Hutchings may have been the first journalist to write about Yosemite; he was not the last, however. Soon other writers accompanied the tourists to Yosemite. Among them were Horace Greeley, editor of the

The Wawona Hotel is built near the site of Galen Clark's hotel, one of the first tourist accommodations in the park. Galen Clark was the park's first guardian.

New York Tribune, and the Reverend Thomas Starr King (for whom Mount Starr King is named) of Boston. Both men wrote of Yosemite's wonders for an eager national audience. Yosemite was compared to the most spectacular European alpine scenery, which until then had been the focus of most American upper-class tourist travel. With its giant sequoias and superb climate, Yosemite quickly became an American icon—a source of pride and attention for the growing young nation.

Along with the writers, increasing numbers of artists and even practicers of the newly invented art of photography came to the valley and recorded their views of it. Among these early chroniclers of Yosemite's visual beauty were photographers C. L. Weed and Carleton E. Watkins, as well as the famous artist Albert Bierstadt. Exhibitions of their work in major cities around the country further enhanced Yosemite's fame.

One of the locals who visited Yosemite in 1855 was Galen Clark (for whom the Clark Range is named). The following year, Clark quit his job with a mining company for health reasons and moved into the mountains along the South Fork of the Merced. He built a rude cabin in some large meadows at present-day Wawona in what would become Yosemite National Park. The following year he discovered the Mariposa grove of sequoias.

Fortunately for Clark, a toll road that passed by his cabin was hastily constructed to the valley, and soon overnight guests were staying with him. Recognizing an opportunity, Clark built a hotel and hosted some of the many travelers who made the trek to the valley in increasing numbers.

Clark was not the only entrepreneur who took advantage of the growing tourist traffic. Two miners, Buck Beardsley and Stephen Cunningham, built a hotel in the valley in the same year. In 1859 another hotel was erected in the upper end of the valley—hence its name, the Upper Hotel.

Besides hotel keepers, settlers took up residence in the valley. James Lamon squatted on land in the upper valley in 1859. He built a cabin and planted a garden and orchards, planning to sell his produce to tourists. James Hutchings bought the Upper Hotel in 1863 and laid claim to a hundred acres in the valley. Under federal homesteading laws, however, neither Lamon nor Hutchings had any legal claim to the land, in part because neither had paid the government the requisite $1.25 an acre required for legal ownership.

Park Protection

The increasing privatization of the valley—legal or otherwise—prompted efforts to protect and preserve it for the public. In 1864 Senator John Conness (for whom Conness Peak is named) introduced legislation into Congress to relinquish federal ownership of the land in the Yosemite Valley and the Mariposa Grove to California to protect as a state park. (What is now Yosemite National Park includes this land, as well as a large area of ridges and alpine basins.) It must be remembered that this was eight years prior to the establishment of Yellowstone National Park. The federal government did not yet have a mechanism for protecting federal lands in the public domain. All the existing laws dealt merely with the transfer of public lands into private hands. In his speech to the Senate, Conness claimed that Yosemite was worthless for any other purpose, since it comprised primarily bare rock and steep terrain. Similar arguments have been used until recently by conservationists arguing for wilderness protection, in an effort to counter opponents who might feel they were losing lands with valuable timber or minerals. As a result of this policy of protecting remote sites, valuable wildlife habitat in more accessible areas has been lost to development, particularly in the lower foothills of the Sierra Nevada. The unfortunate consequences of this kind of argument, however, did not become apparent for decades.

The senator made it clear that the purpose of the bill was the "preservation both of the Yosemite Valley and the Big Tree Grove . . . to be used and preserved for the benefit of mankind." It may not seem like it today, but this was a radical idea for its time, when the federal government's land policies were geared toward getting as much of the public domain into private ownership as possible. Protecting any land, particularly scenery, for the benefit of future generations was a genuine act of forethought and vision. Senator Conness's Yosemite Park Act sailed through Congress, and President Abraham Lincoln signed it into law on June 30, 1864. It was the first legislation in the nation that set aside and protected land primarily for its scenic values.

The Yosemite Park Act directed the state to put together a park commission to guide development and protection of the preserve. Frederick Law Olmsted (for whom Olmsted Point is named), a prominent landscape architect who subsequently designed New York City's Central Park, was named chair of the commission. Galen Clark, another commission member, was named as the first guardian of the park.

Shortly after the formation of the commission, Hutchings, Lamon, and the other valley squatters were given notice that they must give up their holdings or sign a lease to remain in Yosemite. They refused, claiming that the state had no authority over them. The state then began legal proceedings against them for trespassing. The court battle that ensued eventually went all the way to the U.S. Supreme Court. In the Hutchings vs. Low decision of 1872, the court finally ruled against the settler's claims. The case reaffirmed the federal government's right to withdraw lands from settlement and to protect park lands as a public trust.

Nevertheless, by pressing their case Hutchings and the other squatters were able to obtain sixty thousand dollars—a huge sum of money for the day—from sympathetic California legislators as compensation for land they had no legal right to. In the end, they were far better off financially than if they had been given title to the property in the first place.

Though a great deal of national attention was focused on Yosemite, not many people visited it during its early years. Getting to Yosemite was still a lengthy trek. In the nine years between 1855 and 1864, only 653 visitors registered at the hotels in the valley. But this changed when the transcontinental railroad crossed the Sierra in 1869. In that year alone, more than twelve hundred visitors arrived in the valley. A building boom hit. A small hotel was even built on a ledge between Vernal and Nevada falls, and another, known as Mountain House, was constructed at the end of the trail to Glacier Point. Overdevelopment of the Yosemite Valley is not just a modern dilemma; it began in the park's earliest days. Although Congress initially made it clear that private real estate was no longer permitted in Yosemite National Park, problems with overdevelopment by concessionaires have continued to plague the park right up to the present.

One of the most ardent proponents of strict protection was the Yosemite Park Commission's chair, Frederick Law Olmsted. In a report he authored in 1865, Olmsted predicted that the number of people visiting the park would rise from a few hundred to "become thousands and in a century the whole number of visitors will be counted in the millions." He went on to argue that it was the duty of the commission to protect the "rights of posterity as well as of contemporary visitors," for "the millions who are hereafter to benefit by the Act have the largest interest in it, and the largest interest should be first and most strenuously guarded." Unfortunately for Yosemite, the report was suppressed by other members of the commission, and Olmsted's recommendations were never implemented. He resigned as chair soon after.

John Muir

Yosemite's greatest champion was John Muir. A lean, spare man with clear, blue eyes and a thick beard, Muir fit the popular image of Jesus Christ. Certainly the fervor and enthusiasm with which he continuously sang the praises of wildness and natural things would be called religious by today's standards. But Muir was more than a disciple of the wilderness; he was the most eloquent spokesperson of his day for the preservation of natural integrity.

Many of Muir's ideas were religious in tone, for he thought that nature was the outward manifestion of God. He used this theme repeatedly in his writings. To Muir, the Sierra Nevada was sacred ground, as holy as the sacred sites Indians revered in other parts of the North American landscape.

And if the landscape was sacred, then so were the plants and animals living upon it. Muir anticipated the arguments of the animal rights movement by a hundred years. He argued passionately that hunting was of questionable ethics. "The murder business . . . has been pushed ruthlessly, merrily on, until at last protective measures are being called for, partly, I suppose, because the pleasure of killing is in danger of being lost from there being little or nothing left to kill, and partly, let us hope, from a dim glimmering recognition of the rights of animals and their kinship to ourselves." On a trip in Yosemite with then President Theodore Roosevelt, a renowned hunter, Muir chided the president by asking him, "Mr. Roosevelt, when are you going to get beyond the boyishness of killing things . . . are you not getting far enough along to leave that off?"

Muir's concern was not limited to animals. In castigating the cut-and-run tactics of loggers, Muir wrote, "Any fool can destroy trees. They cannot run away; and if they could, they would still be destroyed . . . God has cared for these trees, saved them from drought, disease, avalanches, and a thousand straining leveling tempests and floods; but he cannot save them from fools."

Anticipating the ideas of today's conservation biologists, Muir recognized that everything in nature is connected. He continuously argued for the preservation of large tracts of unfragmented wilderness, realizing intuitively that only large parcels of the landscape could reasonably assure long-term ecological integrity. "For the branching canyons and valleys of the basin of the streams that pour into Yosemite are as closely related to it as are the fingers to the palm of the hand—as the branches, foliage, and flowers of a tree to the trunk." As a consequence of this realization, Muir argued forcefully for protecting entire drainages, not just single valleys. In advocating the preservation of Yosemite he wrote, "all the fountain region above Yosemite, with its peaks, canyons, snowfields, glaciers, forests, and streams, should be included in the park to make it an harmonious unit instead of a fragment, great though the fragment be."

Muir was not a native of the western landscape he revered. He was born in Scotland and raised on a stump farm in Wisconsin. A promising inventor, he enrolled at the University of Wisconsin and spent several years there but never graduated. Instead, he left to seek a broader education in the "university of the wilderness" as he called it. He walked a thousand miles from Indiana to Florida. But when he was stricken by malaria, he abandoned plans for a trip to South America. Instead he booked passage on a boat to California.

Early Years in Yosemite

In March 1868 Muir arrived in San Francisco. He immediately left town for Yosemite—a place he had read about. He spent eight days in the valley and was captivated. In the Sierra, which he dubbed the "Range of Light," Muir found his heaven on earth. The best part of heaven was the valley known as Yosemite. "No temple made with hands can compare with Yosemite," he wrote; this was "the grandest of all the special temples of Nature."

After Muir's brief visit, he returned to the foothills and worked as a ferry operator, sheepherder, and bronc buster. In May 1869 rancher Pat Delaney offered Muir the opportunity to spend a summer in the mountains. All Delaney wanted was someone reliable to accompany his sheep and sheepherder and to make sure neither wandered off. Muir would be free to study the flora, fauna, and rocks, or whatever took his fancy.

Muir accompanied the sheep up through the forests between the Merced and Tuolumne river drainages all the way to the meadows at Tuolumne. He spent the summer working out his early theories of glaciation, botanizing, and exploring. He had time to climb Mount Dana and Cathedral Peak and hiked down Bloody Canyon to Mono Lake.

After this initial contact, Muir knew he had to spend more time in the Sierra, so once the herds were taken back to the Central Valley for the winter, he got a job in Yosemite Valley operating a sawmill. His boss was the innkeeper James Hutchings. Muir designed a water-powered mill and cut wind-toppled trees (he refused to cut down a live tree) into boards for use in the Hutchings hotel and home. He built a small, snug cabin for himself along Yosemite Creek and diverted a portion of the current into his cabin so he could hear it "sing and warble in low, sweet tones, delightful at night while I lay in bed."

Glacial Scientist

The work was not demanding. It left Muir a lot of time to explore the valley. Muir was not yet a vocal advocate for conservation, although he had already developed a strong love of nature. Rather, his Yosemite rambles were often motivated by his love of science, especially geology. As Muir saw more of Yosemite Valley and the Sierran high country, he became convinced that glaciers had carved many of the magnificent features, including the broad, sculpted valley. Of Yosemite's glacial origins, Muir wrote, "Nature chose for a tool not the earthquake or eroding rain, but the tender snow-flowers noiselessly falling through unnumbered centuries. . . . In united strength they crushed and ground and wore away the rocks in their march."

Such a view was contrary to the accepted notions of the day that attributed the formation of Yosemite Valley to a giant cataclysmic earthquake. In particular, Muir's theories about glaciation countered the opinions of Josiah Whitney (for whom Mount Whitney is named), head of the California Geological Survey. A rancorous debate over Yosemite's origins continued for years. Whitney attempted to discredit Muir by branding him an "ignoramus" and "mere sheepherder." Clarence King, another member of the Survey, cautioned others, "It is hoped that Mr. Muir's vagaries will not deceive geologists who are personally unacquainted with California," and called Muir an "ambitious amateur."

Despite this criticism, Muir soon garnered the support of Louis Agassiz, the premier geologist of his day. Agassiz described Muir as "the first man who has any adequate conception of glacial action." In addition, when Joseph LeConte, a geology professor from the newly established University of California at Berkeley, and a group of college students stopped at the Hutchings sawmill to ask directions, they were immediately impressed by the man in "rough miller's garb, whose intelligent face and earnest, clear blue eyes excited our interest." When they learned that they were talking to John Muir, of whom they had already heard, they invited him to accompany their expedition to the Yosemite high country. This was just the sort of adventure Muir loved, and he eagerly accepted. Muir and LeConte became close friends, and later that year LeConte published several papers that supported Muir's glacier theories.

Muir's ideas gained even greater acceptance in 1871 after he discovered an active glacier in a cirque below Merced Peak. In addition, Muir published accounts of his observations and exploits in popular magazines and newspapers of the day. His "Yosemite Glaciers" was published by the *New York Daily Tribune,* and several other pieces followed. Nevertheless, Whitney continued to denigrate Muir and even suggested that no glaciers existed in the Sierra. Although the details of Muir's theory have proven to be incorrect, the general idea he espoused was closer to the truth than were the ideas of any of his contemporaries. A 1971 study conducted by the U.S. Geological Survey found more than five hundred glaciers in the Sierra. Today the accepted theory for the formation of Yosemite Valley is that stream erosion created the original deep canyon, which was then modified by glacial action.

Despite the condescending remarks of Whitney, King, and others, Muir's fame began to grow, and more than one prominent scientist or leader visiting Yosemite sought him as a guide. Muir's reputation as a scientist as well as a philosopher was growing steadily and he increasingly enjoyed the respect of his peers. In 1871 Ralph Waldo Emerson, one of the most famous writers of the day and one of Muir's heros, arrived in Yosemite and sought the mountaineer out.

Expansion of the Park

Muir's scientific curiosity spanned far more than geology. In 1873 and 1875 he made two trips south of Yosemite to investigate the distribution and ecology of the isolated groves of giant sequoias along the western flank of the Sierra. In 1876 the American Association for the Advancement of Science published a paper Muir wrote describing the tree's ecology and Muir's theory explaining its erratic distribution.

Muir's ramblings in the southern Sierra changed his life. Much of the early conservation work in the Yosemite region occurred without Muir's input. The state park was established four years before he even saw the valley. Even after his arrival, Muir spent more time tramping among the peaks than lobbying for their protection. In the Tule River drainage south of today's Sequoia National Park, however, he found loggers hacking up the ancient sequoia groves, and in Kings Canyon he discovered a sign claiming land for private ownership. Both discoveries were pivotal for him. Muir gave up the life of science he had been leaning toward to become an advocate for the land.

His early experiences with domestic sheep made Muir an adamant anti-livestock crusader. Though he lamented the logging of the Sierras' splendid forests, he considered livestock the greatest threat. Muir described domestic sheep as "hooved locusts." In June 1889 he met with Robert Underwood Johnson, the influential associate editor of *Century*, the nation's leading magazine. Johnson accompanied Muir to Yosemite. They happened to camp in Tuolumne Meadows immediately after a band of sheep had eaten its way through. This launched Muir on a diatribe against sheep. At the time, the only legal way to eliminate livestock from the land was by proclaiming it a national park. Johnson urged Muir to work to exclude livestock from the Sierran high country and agreed to publish anything Muir might write on the subject. In addition, Johnson agreed to work behind the scenes, using his influence to introduce a park bill into Congress.

With that in mind, Muir wrote two articles, "The Treasure of Yosemite" and "Features of the Proposed National Park," advocating the creation of a Yosemite National Park, modeled after Yellowstone. Both articles urged protection for the headwaters of the Tuolumne and Merced rivers as a means of protecting these watersheds from the depredations of domestic livestock. They appeared in *Century* in the summer and fall of 1890.

Ironically, despite the efforts of Muir and Johnson, Yosemite's establishment may have had more to do with economic motives than with altruism. There is convincing evidence that the support of Daniel Zumwalt, a representative of the Southern Pacific Railroad, helped to gain passage of a Yosemite bill. Southern Pacific hoped to profit by transporting tourists to the new park. Furthermore, the bill called for protecting "reserved forest lands" with no mention of a national park. This may have been done to purposely deceive or defuse opponents.

On September 30, 1890, a bill essentially following Muir's recommendations was passed by both Houses of Congress; however, the bill addressed only the lands surrounding Yosemite Valley but not the valley itself, which continued to remain under state control as a state park.

Shortly after the successful campaign to get the Yosemite region set aside as a national park, Muir, along with a number of other prominent Californians, formed the Sierra Club—one of the nation's first environmental organizations. Muir was elected president, a post he held for twenty-two years until his death. The club had two goals. One was to foster exploration and recreation in the mountains; the second was to generate support for the preservation of the Sierra Nevada's forests and rivers. Almost immediately after its formation, the club headed off an attempt to decrease the size of Yosemite to benefit livestock, mining, and timber interests.

Neighboring Forest Reserves

In 1891 a new means of protecting forests was created when Congress passed the Forest Reserve Act, which allowed the president to withdraw forested lands from the public domain for conservation purposes. In 1893 President Benjamin Harrison used the Forest Reserve Act to create a four-million-acre Sierra Forest Reserve that stretched from Yosemite south to the Kern River drainage. This assured that the majority of the central and southern Sierra Nevada would remain in public ownership. Harrison's proclamation signaled a marked reversal of public land policy. Until that time, it had been government practice to transfer as much land as possible to private ownership for exploitation.

At that time, there was virtually no difference between a national park and a forest reserve. Both prohibited most extractive industries including mining, logging, and livestock grazing. The growing conservation movement generally favored public ownership of forests. Muir was a leader in this movement. Other leaders, such as Bernhard Fernow and Gifford Pinchot, turned out to have vastly different perspectives on the ultimate fate of these lands.

Reacting to growing opposition to forest reserves from western mining, grazing, and logging interests, Congress put together a blue-ribbon task force to formulate a philosophy for reserve management. The committee included prominent scientists like Charles Sargent, William Brewer, and Alexander Agassiz; Arnold Hauge of the U.S. Geological Survey; General H. L. Abbott, an engineer; and Gifford Pinchot, a recent graduate of forestry schools in Europe who later became the first director of the U.S. Forest Service.

Pinchot also became the leader of the Wise Use Movement, which advocated "scientific management and use" of the land. Muir, on the other hand, held a less utilitarian perspective. To him, forests and wilderness had values unto themselves, regardless of whether or not they fulfilled immediate resource needs.

Muir joined the other members of the committee in Montana, and they toured the West together. At this time, Pinchot and Muir were in general agreement about the need to create additional forest reserves. Pinchot and Muir became close friends, because as Pinchot later described it, they "both loved the woods."

In the end, the commission split over divergent philosophies. Sargent and Muir thought the goal of the committee should be to recommend additional lands to be protected in an undeveloped state. Pinchot and Hauge thought they were recommending lands that would and should be developed but managed wisely. Muir and Sargent were accused of wanting to lock up valuable resources.

In some ways this was an unfair accusation. Both Muir and Sargent did not oppose timber cutting, grazing, mining, and other activities in some places. Just as he later opposed a dam in Hetch Hetchy Canyon on the Tuolumne River on the grounds that there were alternatives to damming one of the finest canyons in the Sierra, Muir felt that some forests should remain inviolate where alternatives were available. Pinchot and Hauge, on the other hand, thought that scientific management would enhance forests and rangelands, thus producing a product while improving the condition of these lands. As a consequence, they felt there was no need to protect any lands that had the potential of responding to management. In their view, a scientifically managed forest was actually better off than an unmanaged forest.

Interestingly, the committee's debate foreshadowed future conflicts between the present-day Wise Use Movement, which seeks to allow extractive uses on public land, and those interested in restricting development on public land. The preservationist philosophy is based in part on the assumption that the complexity of natural ecosystems exceeds the limits of human knowledge and that this makes it difficult to distinguish wise uses from actions that may have long-term detrimental consequences.

Unfortunately for Muir and Sargent, their perspective did not prevail. In 1897 Congress passed the Forest Management Act, which stated that forest reserves were to provide "a continuous supply of timber for the use and necessities of citizens of the United States." Forest reserves were also opened to mining and livestock grazing.

Pinchot and Muir had a falling out that summer in Seattle. Muir, just returning from a trip to Alaska, read in the Seattle papers that Pinchot endorsed livestock grazing in the forest reserves. To Muir this represented the ultimate compromise; just the previous summer Pinchot had been adamant about the damage that livestock had done to forests. Furthermore, Muir knew from his experiences in the Sierra Nevada that domestic livestock was the major threat to the watersheds, wildlife, and forests of the reserve lands. It was inconceivable to Muir that anyone concerned with conservation would advocate livestock grazing in forest reserves.

The realization that forest reserves would no longer protect mountain ranges like the Sierra converted Muir into an ardent supporter of national parks, in part because they were off limits to livestock use. Pinchot soon co-opted the term "conservation" to mean wise use, prompting wilderness advocates to call him a "de-conservationist." Pinchot continued to trumpet the wise use agenda, however, leaving Muir and other wild land supporters little choice but to split their time and effort battling the wise use utilitarians as well as the less responsible development interests.

Changes in Park Borders

Meanwhile, Muir and the Sierra Club were lobbying to remove Yosemite Valley from state control and to bring it under federal management. In their view the state's park commission had seriously compromised the beauty and integrity of the valley. There were saloons, a post office, a general store, hotels, stables, barns, and art galleries, plus many private dwellings. (In fact, it was not much different from today.) Permission for most of the construction had been granted by the commission in the preceding ten years. In addition, cattle, horses, and even pigs trampled and grazed most of the valley's meadows, and fences broke up the landscape into small pastures where little vegetation remained. After a visit to Yosemite in 1896, Muir commented that the "only flowers left were those on inaccessible ledges and recesses high on the walls."

Muir soon had a chance to bring the deplorable state of the valley to the attention of the nation's highest officer. When President Theodore Roosevelt visited Yosemite in 1903 he requested that Muir accompany him as a guide and companion. Muir joined the presidential entourage in Oakland, traveled by train with the president to Raymond, and then rode in his stage the remainder of the distance to the park. Along the way, Muir informed Roosevelt about the abuses that state control had permitted and urged him to support federal reacquisition of the valley. By the time they reached Yosemite, Muir had convinced Roosevelt that federal control offered better protection for the valley.

Once in the park, Roosevelt, with boyish enthusiasm, asked to get beyond the usual sights and to see the real Yosemite. Abandoning most of the presidential party, Muir and Roosevelt camped out with a few rangers in the backcountry. Circled around a campfire for warmth, they talked late into the night. Muir stuffed the president with his concerns about Yosemite and other issues ranging from forestry management to proposals for additional national parks across the country. That night Roosevelt slept out under the trees with just blankets for warmth. In the morning a fresh snowfall covered him.

It was an experience Roosevelt never forgot. Later he would fondly recall the time he slept "among the pines and silver firs in the Sierra solitude, in a snowstorm, too, and without a tent. I passed one of the pleasantest nights of my life. It was so reviving to be so close to nature in this magnificent forest."

Buoyed by the president's encouragement, Muir and the Sierra Club moved ahead with their efforts to consolidate management of the park. Their efforts were rewarded in 1905 when recession of Yosemite Valley and Mariposa Grove to the federal government was approved by Congress.

After Yosemite Valley came back under federal jurisdiction, some individuals advocated the expansion of park borders. Acting Superintendent Lieutenant Colonel Joseph Garrard noted that "animals leave the higher altitudes as soon as snow comes, and in the lowlands and meadows about the park fall easy prey to the hunter." He reasoned that all federal lands surrounding the park should also be managed to protect wildlife and preserve its habitat. In effect, he argued for a "Greater Yosemite Ecosystem" approach to management of the park and surrounding lands.

Efforts were also afoot, however, to reduce the area of the park. Miners wanted access to mineral-rich lands near the eastern border; loggers eyed the low- and mid-elevation virgin pine forests; and livestock producers continued to covet the grazing lands within the park. Those who supported reductions in the park's area argued that preventing trespass was impossible since one could not readily tell where the park began or ended; furthermore, the locking up of valuable resources hindered the economic growth and development of California. Muir countered these arguments. "The smallest reserve, and the first ever heard of," he wrote, "was in the Garden of Eden, and though its boundaries were drawn by the Lord, and embraced only one tree, yet the rules were violated by the only two settlers that were permitted on suffrage to live in it."

Congress created another commission to address these concerns. It recommended that land be deleted from Yosemite in several areas, including the western boundary between the Merced and Tuolumne rivers, additional forests south of the Merced River, and much of the scenic high country at the headwaters of the San Joaquin River in and around the Minarets.

The Sierra Club, meanwhile, submitted a proposal to the commission recommending expansion of the park's borders, particularly along the eastern divide, to encompass lands beyond Tioga Pass and as far east as the town of Mammoth Lakes.

The commission rejected the Sierra Club's recommendations except for the addition of lands to the north of the Tuolumne River, but they held tight to their initial recommendations to reduce the park's borders on the west, southwest, and southeast boundaries. In February 1905 President Roosevelt signed into law a bill that redrew the boundaries of the park in accordance with the commission's recommendations. The end result was a significant reduction in the low-elevation lands sought as winter range by wildlife, which today would add considerably to the biological richness of Yosemite.

Another reduction of the park was approved near Wawona in 1906, and logging proceeded in this quarter almost immediately. Acting Superintendent Major H. C. Benson noted with alarm in 1908 that "game is on the decrease. Each reduction of the park has cut another portion of the winter resort of game." Altogether the boundary changes made to accommodate transportation corridors, logging, mining, and grazing reduced the park's area by one-third.

Some of this loss was reversed in 1930 when 12,000 acres straddling the land between the Tuolumne and Merced sequoia groves were purchased using funds from the federal government and matching funds provided by John D. Rockefeller. In 1932 another 8,765 acres near Wawona were purchased and added to the park. The Carl Inn Tract, a parcel adjacent to the Rockefeller addition, was added in 1937 and 1939.

Hetch Hetchy

At the same time that Muir and the Sierra Club were fighting to protect Yosemite from any further reductions in size, the city of San Francisco petitioned the federal government to construct a dam in Hetch Hetchy Canyon on the Tuolumne River within the park. The initial application was filed in 1901 and rejected in 1903 because Secretary of the Interior Ethan Allen Hitchcock felt it was "not in keeping with the public interest." But the issue was not dead.

After the devastation created by the massive 1906 San Francisco Earthquake and the resulting fires, San Francisco immediately reapplied for a permit to construct a dam in Hetch Hetchy Canyon. Public sympathy for the city weighed heavily in Secretary of the Interior James Garfield's 1908 decision to grant the permit. In defending his decision, Garfield noted, "Domestic use is the highest use to which water and available storage basins . . . can be put."

John Muir, who considered the spectacular, cliff-walled Hetch Hetchy Canyon to be a "second Yosemite," strongly disagreed. "Dam Hetch Hetchy! As well dam for watertanks the people's cathedrals and churches, for no holier temple has ever been consecrated by the heart of man." He, along with longtime ally Robert Underwood Johnson, launched a nationwide campaign to save the canyon.

Upon learning of San Francisco's application, Muir wrote President Roosevelt, reminding him of the beauty of Yosemite they had experienced together and requesting that the president oppose the dam. Roosevelt was sympathetic to Muir's concerns, for he also was a lover of wild country. In his letter Muir suggested there were alternative sites available; however, Secretary Garfield reported to the president that no suitable alternatives were as cost effective.

Besides support for the project from his interior secretary, Roosevelt was also influenced by Gifford Pinchot. Pinchot, now director of the U.S. Forest Service, and one of Roosevelt's closest friends and confidants, expressed support for the dam project. It was not that Pinchot did not appreciate Hetch Hetchy's beauty; rather, his commitment to utilitarian goals prevented him from opposing the project. In his letter to the president, Pinchot wrote, "I believe the highest possible use which could be made of it would be to supply pure water to a great center of population." Pinchot's decision reflected his philosophy of providing "the greatest good for the greatest number of people." To Pinchot, it was clear that a dependable water supply for San Francisco outweighed any value the Hetch Hetchy Canyon might have to the handful of nature lovers who might visit it. Roosevelt, bowing to Pinchot's influence, reluctantly refused Muir's request to oppose the dam.

As with the issue of opening up the forest reserves to mining, logging, and grazing, Hetch Hetchy became a battleground between two different philosophies of land use. Arguing against the dam before a Congressional hearing, Johnson protested "against the materialistic idea that there must be something wrong about a man who finds one of the highest uses of nature in the fact that it is made to be looked at." Lyman Abbott, editor of *Outlook* magazine, argued against the dam, suggesting that the "national habit is to waste the beauty of Nature and save the dollars of business."

As the campaign heightened, the Sierra Club and Appalachian Mountain Club prepared a brochure that outlined the major points against the dam and discussed alternative reservoir sites. Even Roosevelt had second thoughts about his original support for the project; in an annual message to the nation in 1908, he declared in reference to Yosemite that "all wild things should be protected and the scenery kept wholly unmarred." The publicity strategy stalled but did not stop the efforts to dam the Tuolumne.

Finally, in 1913 the House Committee on Public Lands held a hearing on the Hetch Hetchy dam permit, and Gifford Pinchot appeared as a staunch proponent of the reservoir. He asked the committee to consider "whether the advantage of leaving this valley in a state of nature is greater than . . . using it for the benefit of the city of San Francisco."

When the vote finally came up before the House, the decision to grant the dam permit won; however, before the Senate acted on the matter the dam, opponents had mobilized. Editorials in leading magazines and newspapers all around the country took up the matter. Many opposed the dam, including the *New York Times, Outlook, Collier's, Nation,* and others. One Utah senator got five thousand letters in opposition to the dam.

Like current issues such as endangered species protection, the Hetch Hetchy conflict was oversimplified. Proponents predicted that people would die in San Francisco because the city would not have enough water to fight fires. On the other hand, conservationists thought there were other options that could satisfy San Francisco's water needs without destroying one of the most spectacular and wild valleys in the Sierra.

In the end, the dam proponents won out, and the Senate approved the permit. President Woodrow Wilson signed the bill into law on December 19, 1913. Muir, though dejected, could take some consolation from the fact that there had been a national debate about the Sierran valley at all. For most of the history of the country up to that point had been one of trying to tame the wilderness and develop it as rapidly as possible. To have the nation stop and consider whether there might be merit to preserving some landscapes for their intrinsic values was a significant and profound change in its collective attitudes.

Early Wildlife Management

For John Muir and others, one of the major reasons for setting aside Yosemite National Park was to preserve natural habitat for wildlife. Yet, during the early years of the park, management was based upon notions of "good" and "bad" animals. Predators like mountain lion, wolverine, fox, lynx, and coyote were trapped either to rid the park of animals considered a nuisance, or merely for their furs, which provided supplemental income for park rangers. Trapping of furbearers by park rangers continued until 1925, and predator control went beyond this date. For instance, the park superintendent proudly reported that the state lion hunter had killed forty-three mountain lions in Yosemite in 1927 alone, and more than four hundred had been killed by this man since he began his Yosemite lion hunting efforts. Hawks (bad animals) like the Cooper's hawk and sharp-shinned hawk were shot because they preyed on songbirds (good animals). These raptors no longer breed in Yosemite Valley, although they once did. Other animals like rattlesnakes were killed on sight—to make Yosemite "safer" for people. Grizzly bears were wiped out throughout the entire Sierra and eventually California for much the same reason.

Eventually, many people came to object to such policies. For example, Joseph Grinnell, a professor at U.C. Berkeley, coauthored an article with Tracy Storer that appeared in *Science Magazine*. The authors argued that the "supreme value in national parks" was that they "furnished samples of the Earth as it was before the advent of the white man." They were, in other words, natural laboratories or controls against which we could compare the areas we manipulated.

Demonstrating an early appreciation of the fact that nothing in nature is wasted, they noted that "even down timber is an essential factor in upholding the balance of animal life, for fallen and decaying logs provide homes for wild rats and mice of various kinds, and these in turn support many carnivorous birds and mammals, such as hawks, owls, foxes and martens."

Even more bold was their plea to protect native predators that for a long time had been killed within Yosemite by National Park Service rangers as a matter of park policy. Grinnell and Storer argued that "predaceous animals should be left unmolested and allowed to retain their primitive relation to the rest of the fauna, even though this may entail a consider-able annual levy on the animals forming their prey."

Besides attempting to eradicate native species, it was also park policy to introduce "desirable" species. Trout, never found above the 4,000-foot level, were introduced into many high-elevation lakes and streams. This had serious consequences for other native species such as frogs, whose numbers began to decline due to predation on tadpoles by the introduced fish.

Another ill-conceived project was an attempt to introduce Tule elk into Yosemite. Never native to Yosemite itself, Tule elk had once been common among the riparian areas of the Central Valley. Agricultural development combined with market hunting reduced their numbers, however, to the point where they faced imminent extinction. A proposal to place elk in Yosemite was welcomed by the Park Service as a way of increasing visitation. A twenty-eight-acre fenced enclosure was built in the Yosemite Valley. A dozen elk were placed in their new home. Eventually, the animals were removed to a location in the Owens Valley east of the Sierra where they are still found today.

Though the grizzly bear was extirpated from the Sierra, its smaller cousin the black bear has survived. By the 1930s bears were a regular feature of Yosemite Park visits. The concessionaires built viewing platforms, and each evening garbage was spread out to attract bears, while buses were run from the hotels to carry tourists to the feeding pits. Naturally, as more bears were attracted to the valley for food, there was a marked increase in bear-human problems. Bears did not confine their foraging to the feeding pits. Campgrounds were raided, and people were injured. In 1929, for example, eighty-one people were treated for bear injuries in the park. Some people and officials began to wonder if Yosemite was being "administered for the use and enjoyment of the people or the use and enjoyment of the bears." Of course, such remarks never acknowledged that the problem was created by people.

To deal with the bear situation, offending animals were usually trapped, marked with white paint, and released in other parts of the park. If they got into trouble a second time, they were killed. It was not until 1940 that the Park Service halted the bear feeding shows. Yet bear deaths did not stop. Between 1960 and 1972, more than two hundred bears were destroyed by the Park Service within Yosemite.

On rare occasions, bears are still killed in Yosemite, but the Park Service's emphasis has shifted. It has intensified its efforts to educate visitors about keeping food away from bears. Regulations that attempt to minimize bear habituation to food are enforced. People who leave coolers out on picnic tables and campers who neglect to hang or put away their food are fined. The goal is to keep bears wild—thereby reducing conflicts and the likelihood that a bear will be killed.

In an effort to restore natural interactions and wildlife to the park, the agency no longer stocks high-elevation lakes with fish. If the populations die out, they are not replaced. Similarly, bighorn sheep, extirpated long ago as a consequence of unrestricted market hunting and diseases introduced by domestic livestock, have recently been reintroduced to the eastern portion of the park. Research on other wildlife, including red fox, great gray owl, and wolverine, has begun in an effort to determine how best to protect these species or in some cases restore them to the park. These changes in policies, along with greater attention to the restoration of natural ecological processes like fire, bode well for the future of the park's native species.

Concessionaires

David Curry and his wife Jennie were schoolteachers who came to Yosemite in 1899 and set up a few tents for guests against the cliffs below Glacier Point. They revived the firefall, an event in which burning logs were tossed off the cliffs at Glacier Point each evening, to descend in a red cascade to the valley below. This was a great success, particularly from the Currys' perspective since their camp was strategically located beneath Glacier Point.

From this modest beginning, the Curry Company came to dominate Yosemite's politics for decades. At every turn, David Curry (and after his death, his wife) sought to expand operations, often against the wishes of park superintendents and officials. Curry knew how to manipulate public opinion, however, and used his friends in high places to get much, if not all, that he wanted. He justified continual expansion of his business by arguing that it met the so-called needs of park visitors, even if the services already existed elsewhere in the valley.

In 1916 Curry wrote Secretary of the Interior Franklin Lane to argue that more development was necessary to extend the tourist season and thereby the profits of concessionaires like Curry. He wrote "that it was absolutely necessary to extend the season to six months." To do this he suggested building golf courses, reestablishing the firefall, and constructing a dam on Yosemite Creek so that the flow of Yosemite Falls, which tended to dry up in summer, could be regulated and controlled throughout the tourist season.

The Curry Company joined its rival, the Yosemite Park Company, in 1925. The newly established Yosemite Park and Curry Company continued its efforts to expand services in every way imaginable. Everything from swimming pools, golf courses, and ice skating rinks to the ski area at Badger Pass to bearbaiting was justified as fulfilling some necessity or need. None of these uses could be construed as being consistent with the original purpose and intent of a national park. The concessionaires aspired to make Yosemite like anyplace else, but with waterfalls.

The Eternal Debate

People have been lamenting the impacts of visitation on park values practically since Yosemite was established. At first most people, even John Muir and members of the Sierra Club, viewed increasing visitation as a positive sign. In 1876 Muir wrote, "however frivolous and inappreciative the poorer specimens (of visitors) may appear, viewed comprehensively they are a most hopeful sign of the times, indicating at least the beginning of our return to nature—for going to the mountains is going home." As a consequence, in its early years the Sierra Club encouraged the development and construction of new roads to facilitate visitation and generate support for national parks.

The National Park Service's first director, Stephen Mather, also encouraged visitation and promoted parks as recreational areas. After private automobiles were permitted to enter Yosemite in 1913, visitation increased rapidly. Between 1914 and 1918, the number of annual park visitors increased from 15,154 to 35,527. The car democratized Yosemite and made it accessible to the masses. By 1929, more than 461,000 people came to Yosemite per year.

By 1992, more than 3.5 million people visited Yosemite annually. Yet despite the crowding, most people's experience of Yosemite is positive. Even with the many structures built in the valley, in some ways Yosemite is wilder now than it once was. Cattle and horses no longer trample the meadows. Camping and driving in the meadows, standard practices from 1910 to the 1930s, are now prohibited. Human trails are controlled, and many of the meadows are recovering from excessive use. Hunting, which continued into the twentieth century, no longer occurs within the park. Large pine trees are no longer cut for building materials. And fire, once banned from fulfilling its natural role, is now being reintroduced into the valley.

In some ways, you could say Yosemite is better off now than it once was. Nevertheless, it is still a long way from what it could be.

Today there are thirteen hundred buildings in the valley and seventeen acres of land are under parking lots.

Despite misinformation to the contrary, the greatest impact on trail and backcountry results not from backpackers but from horse use, such as in this packtrain along Rafferty Creek. Studies have shown that one horse does the same damage as ten to twenty-five backpackers.

In 1980 the Park Service issued its General Management Plan. It called for reduction of overnight accommodations by 17 percent and reduction of employee housing by 68 percent. It proposed moving park and concessionaire administrative facilities out of the valley and removing the tennis courts, golf courses, and ice skating rinks. All this was to be accomplished by 1990.

As of 1992 few of these proposals had been implemented. Overnight accommodations had increased, employee housing had been cut by only 14 percent, and most administrative facilities remained in the valley.

It remains to be seen whether Yosemite Valley will ever be returned to a nearly pristine state resembling what the Indians and earliest visitors knew. It is not even clear whether most park visitors would find this desirable.

The problems besetting Yosemite are not unique. The difficulties of maintaining natural ecosystems while permitting human uses would challenge even King Solomon. Nevertheless, the trend is clear. Yosemite is not as it was in 1851, but it's a lot closer to this goal than it was even as recently as twenty years ago, in spite of increasing visitation.

Much of the credit for this restoration lies with the National Park Service, whose management is increasingly geared toward preservation of wild lands. But even the most well-intentioned federal employees need to be monitored and, on occasion, chided or goaded into action. Numerous environmental groups, including national organizations like the Sierra Club and the Wilderness Society and local groups such as the California Wilderness Coalition, fulfill this watchdog role. These organizations and the National Park Service strive to achieve the appropriate balance for Yosemite. If we can't solve the conflict between human use and preservation of wild lands here, then it's unlikely we can solve it anywhere else.

Chronology of Important Events

1776: Sierra Nevada named by Spaniard Pedro Font.

1806: Merced River named by Morago expedition exploring Central Valley.

1833: Party of Joseph Walker, American fur trapper, crosses Sierra Nevada, passing through the future Yosemite National Park.

1848: Gold discovered in foothills of Sierra Nevada sets off a mass migration to California.

1850: Gold rush to Mariposa region. Indians attack James Savage's trading posts.

1851: Mariposa Battalion tracks Indians to Yosemite Valley. First whites enter the valley.

1852: Death of miners at hands of Indians in valley prompts retaliation; Indians driven across Sierra to Mono Lake.

1854: James Capen ("Grizzly") Adams traps several grizzlies in Yosemite.

1855: James Mason Hutchings, writer and tourist, first visits the valley.

1857: Galen Clark, Yosemite's first guardian, settles at Wawona and discovers Mariposa sequoia grove.

1863: The Whitney Geological Survey party visits Yosemite, naming many features of the park.

1864: Hutchings takes over Upper Hotel. Yosemite Valley and Mariposa Grove deeded to state of California as public park.

1868: John Muir first sees Yosemite.

1869: John Muir makes first ascent of Cathedral Peak.

1871: First ascent of Mount Lyell, Yosemite's highest peak. Muir publishes his first article, "Yosemite Glaciers."

1872: Lone Pine Earthquake shakes Yosemite. Supreme Court reaffirms that Yosemite must be managed as a national trust.

1874: Colterville Road reaches Yosemite Valley.

1876: Muir publishes anti-livestock article, the first of many attacking the industry.

1880: Hutchings appointed guardian of Yosemite.

1882: Construction begins on Great Sierra Wagon Road (Tioga Pass road).

1885: John Lembert homesteads in Tuolumne Meadows.

1886: John Murphy homesteads at Tenaya Lake.

1889: John Muir and Robert Underwood Johnson camp in Tuolumne Meadows, hatching idea for Yosemite National Park.

1890: Yosemite National Park established by act of Congress.

1891: U.S. Cavalry assigned to Yosemite to supervise park protection.

1892: Sierra Club formed in San Francisco with John Muir as first president.

1893: Four-million-acre Sierra Forest Reserve established.

1899: Currys establish camp below Glacier Point.

1903: Theodore Roosevelt visits John Muir in Yosemite.

1905: Yosemite reduced in size. California gives valley and Mariposa Grove back to federal government.

1908: San Francisco applies for permit to build dam in Hetch Hetchy Canyon.

1913: First legal entry of automobiles into Yosemite Valley. Congress authorizes construction of O'Shaughnessy Dam on Tuolumne River in Hetch Hetchy Canyon.

1914: John Muir dies.

1915: Tioga Road purchased and given to park.

1916: Congress establishes National Park Service.

1935: Badger Pass Ski Area developed.

1958: First successful climb of El Capitan.

1968: Firefall abolished.

1970: Prescribed burning begins.

1980: General Management Plan released.

1984: Yosemite named World Heritage Site. Ninety-four percent of Yosemite designated wilderness.

1990: Forest fires burn across Yosemite.

GEOLOGY

From its discovery, Yosemite was best known for its geological wonders—rocky cliffs, domes, glacial lakes, and deep valleys. Indeed, it is Yosemite's geological history, more than any other factor, that has contributed to its fame as well as its preservation.

Interpreting the geology of this region is not easy. A great deal of Yosemite's geological history is hidden deep in the earth where we can't see it. Furthermore, erosion has stripped away many layers of the past geologic record. As a consequence, geology is based upon conjecture as much as "rock-solid" evidence, and interpretations are continually changing. This is the story of Yosemite's geological history as we understand it today.

The basin occupied by Upper McCabe Lake was scooped out by glaciers.

Types of Rocks

Rocks are classified according to their origins as igneous, sedimentary, or metamorphic.

Igneous rock, "of fire," is solidified magma, or molten rock. When magma rises from deep within the earth and is spewed out in a volcanic eruption, the resulting igneous rock is extrusive. If the magma never reaches the surface and slowly solidifies in place, it is known as intrusive. The granites of Yosemite are intrusive igneous rocks that formed beneath earth's surface and have since been thrust up into view.

Sedimentary rocks are composed, as their name suggests, of sediments, typically mud or sand that has settled out of water. Sand dunes formed on land can also be transformed into sedimentary rock. Most sedimentary rocks are layered and, when still in their original position, display horizontal banding. Familiar sedimentary rocks include sandstone, mudstone, and limestone.

The third major type is *metamorphic* rock, from two Greek words, *meta*, "change," and *morphe*, "form." These are rocks that have changed, usually as a result of heat and pressure. Both igneous and sedimentary rocks can become metamorphic rocks. Limestone changed by pressure and heat becomes marble, for example, and metamorphosed shale becomes slate. Many of the rocks exposed along Yosemite's western margin in the Merced River valley are metamorphic. They still display the original layering that betrays their sedimentary origins.

Plate Tectonics and Volcanism

Plate tectonics is a theory that explains how the different types of rocks were formed. It holds that the earth is composed of a dozen or so major plates and numerous minor ones that float on the molten rock that makes up the mantle. For instance, North America is composed largely of one plate. Africa is another. The Pacific Ocean basin makes up a third.

These plates are in continuous motion. Some plates are moving apart from one another, others collide or slide past one another. It is thought that rising magma in the earth creates currents in the mantle that pull and shove the plates on its surface.

When continental plates move apart, ocean basins are created in between them. When this happens molten rock pours out of cracks in the earth's crust to create new ocean floor. At the same time, other parts of the basin may be consumed by sliding under a continental plate. For example, 205 million years ago, nearly all of the present continents were united into a supercontinent called Pangaea. Since then, they have split apart, with North and South America moving westward away from Europe and Africa, while the Atlantic Ocean has been created between them.

Most oceanic plates are composed of basalt, a heavy, dense rock; continents are largely underlain by lighter, granitic rock. Some plates are composed of both continental and oceanic materials. For instance, the North American plate includes not only the North American continent but also the western portion of the North Atlantic Ocean.

When an oceanic plate collides with a continental plate, the heavier oceanic material is usually subducted beneath the lighter continental rocks. As it dives deeper into the earth's mantle, the rock melts, and the molten magma rises upward through the continental plate toward the surface, where it may erupt as a volcano. The line of volcanoes that stretches north from Mount Lassen and Mount Shasta in northern California marks the intersection of two colliding plates in the Pacific Northwest.

By subduction, and subsequent mixture and movement of magma, new rocks are created just as older rock mixtures are destroyed. In essence, the earth is continuously recycling its rocks. Thus the sedimentary, igneous, or metamorphic rocks that are now exposed in the Sierra Nevada may have at one time in the past been part of different formations.

The boundary between two major plates is represented by a fault. The San Andreas Fault is California's most famous fault. It marks the border between the North American and the Pacific plates, which are sliding past each other at a rate of about 5.3 centimeters a year. This movement is not always smooth; it is often accomplished in fits and jumps—which we recognize as earthquakes.

Smaller faults often delineate mountain ranges. The eastern slope of the Sierra Nevada has been uplifted along a series of faults that extends more or less north and south along the entire eastern escarpment of the range. Occasionally, the Sierra Nevada is racked by a large earthquake, as it was in 1872 when vertical displacement of as much as seventeen feet occurred in one movement. In 1980 Mammoth Lakes east of Yosemite felt an earthquake that registered 6.1 on the Richter Scale, indicating that the Sierra is still rising. Vertical displacement along the eastern Sierra has been as much as sixteen thousand feet!

Geological History of the Sierra Nevada

The oldest exposed rocks in the Sierra Nevada are approximately 475 million years in age. They were formed during the Paleozoic Era, when what would later become Yosemite National Park lay near the western margin of what we now call the North American continent. Originally sediments deposited in marine environments, these rocks—primarily limestones, sandstones, and shales—were transformed by pressure and heat into metamorphic rocks such as slate, schist, hornfels, and marble.

Then during the Mesozoic Era, about 225 million years ago, the giant continent Pangaea, of which North America was a part, began to break up. North America broke away from Europe and started its westward drift, with the Atlantic Ocean opening in its wake. North America's western edge soon encountered an oceanic plate. Forced to dive beneath the North American plate, the oceanic plate was gradually subsumed and melted. The resulting molten magma rose toward the surface. A string of volcanoes erupted, spewing forth ash and lava over the older Paleozoic deposits and creating what are known as metavolcanic rocks.

Not all of the oceanic plate was subducted, however. Some of the sea floor rocks were scraped off the leading edge of the plate. Welded onto the western margin of the North American plate, they now appear as the serpentine outcrops common along the western flank of the central and northern Sierra. The cherts exposed in the Merced River canyon west of Yosemite National Park also owe their origins to such an event.

About 150 million years ago, the North American plate increased the speed of its westward drift, forcing up a mountain range nearly fifteen thousand feet. This range was composed of the twisted and folded segments of the ocean floor scraped onto adjacent pieces of the continental plate. Over time, these rocks were metamorphosed. Sedimentary rocks, including sandstone, limestone, shale, and conglomerates, contributed to the metamorphic rocks in Yosemite. In addition, some volcanic rocks have also been metamorphosed.

Today we find these rocks exposed in the great gold-bearing metamorphic belt, the Mother Lode country that marks the western margin of the range. As visitors approach Yosemite from the west on Highway 140 along the Merced River, they can view many fine outcrops of these ancient rocks exposed along the canyon. The banded layers of chert that are exposed reveal the marine origins of these sedimentary rocks.

This view of Half Dome from Mount Hoffman shows the generally sloping surface of the Sierra Nevada. After the range was uplifted, most of this westward-tilting plateau was eroded, carving the deep canyons that now separate the otherwise nearly uniform slope.

Another metamorphic belt lies along the eastern edge of Yosemite, running from Twin Lakes north of the park south to Mounts Ritter and Banner in the Minarets. Most of these metamorphic rocks were originally extruded from volcanoes, although some sedimentary formations were also metamorphosed. Metavolcanic outcrops occur among many of the higher peaks in Yosemite; these include the reddish rocks that cap the summits of Mount Dana and Mount Gibbs and those by Ellery Lake at the head of Lee Vining Canyon beyond Tioga Pass. Banded metasedimen-

Near the headwaters of Lewis Creek, Mount Florence rises an imposing 12,561 feet.

tary (metamorphic sedimentary) rocks are exposed near Saddlebag Lake east of the park border a few miles north of Tioga Pass.

These metamorphic rocks once covered all the bedrock that makes up the heart of the Sierra Nevada; however, uplift of the mountains has permitted erosion to strip away most of the old metamorphic rocks and expose the granitic rocks beneath. Today less than 5 percent of the rocks exposed in Yosemite are metamorphic; nearly all the park's outcrops are granitic.

Unlike most of Yosemite, the rock exposed in Mount Dana (below left) and Mount Gibbs (below right) is not granite but part of the eastern metamorphic zone.

Granitic Rock

Granite is a specific kind of rock, but the term is used to refer to all granitic intrusive rocks exposed in the Sierra Nevada. The type of intrusive granitic rock depends on the relative proportions of three major mineral components—quartz, potassium feldspar, and plagioclase. Kinds of granitic rock commonly found in Yosemite include granodiorite, quartz monzonite, quartz monzodiorite, and quartz diorite. Granodiorite contains twice as much plagioclase as granite. Diorite is nearly all plagioclase with little quartz and potassium feldspar. Because the differences are not easily discerned by casual observation, "granite" will suffice for all of these granitic rocks.

The degree of crystallization varies among granitic rocks. Some of the rocks in Yosemite have crystals up to two to three inches across embedded in the rock matrix; these are called phenocrysts. Such large crystals are obvious in the granitic rocks on Johnson Peak and near the headwaters of Rafferty Creek by Vogelsang High Sierra Camp. These intrusions develop in two stages. First, molten magma rises partway to the surface, where it stalls and cools very slowly. Slow cooling leads to the formation of large crystals. Then, this crystal-laden magma is pushed up through the bedrock until it nears the surface, where the remainder of the mixture cools more rapidly, resulting in fine-grained rocks that surround the larger crystals still embedded in the matrix.

In other places dark, rounded football-like bodies of diorite, often oriented in the same direction, are mixed among the lighter granitic rocks. It is thought that these are remnants of pre-existing rocks that were swallowed by the intruding magma but did not completely melt into the mixture. This type of diorite intrusion is evident in the granitic rocks near Arch Rock by the park entrance along the Merced River.

The granitic rocks exposed in Yosemite have their origins in plate movements that began as much as 210 million years ago and continued until approximately 80 million years ago. Magma created by plate collisions formed hundreds of plutons, which can be thought of as blobs of rising hot rock. This molten rock rose into the overlying metamorphic rocks.

Some of this magma reached the surface and erupted from volcanoes as ash, cinders, or lava, depending upon the amount of water and gas mixed in with the molten rock. These volcanoes formed a line of cones similar to the Cascades of today. But where the molten rock failed to reach the

Most granites have mineral grains of nearly equal size; however, some contain
a matrix of fine grains mixed with larger crystals known as phenocrysts.
The slower the molten rock cools, the larger the crystals, as evidenced in this
boulder near Tuolumne Pass in the Cathedral Range.

surface, blobs of magma coalesced and solidified into batholiths. Most of the granitic rocks exposed in Yosemite today were formed in this way nearly six miles below the earth's surface.

The 3,000-foot granite cliffs of El Capitan, towering over the Merced River, are among the highest in the world.

A batholith is not a uniform body; it is composed of many plutons with different chemical and physical properties that affect their outward appearance and form. The breaks between different plutons are evident in the Yosemite Valley. The granites that make up El Capitan form cliffs, while the rock immediately to the west, formed from a different pluton, crumbles into angular blocks deposited as talus at the base of the cliff. More than fifty plutons have been located by geologists within the Yosemite National Park region alone.

Granite Plutons

The oldest pluton bodies occur along the Merced River gorge west of the Yosemite Valley and are believed to have been emplaced 114 million years ago. Then 108 million years ago, another intrusion of granite, called the El Capitan pluton, was emplaced. It now makes up much of the midsection of the Yosemite Valley, including its namesake, El Capitan, as well as Cathedral Rocks and the Three Brothers. An even younger intrusion, the Taft granite, invaded the El Capitan pluton. It is exposed at Dewey Point and elsewhere. At 87 million years of age, the Half Dome granodiorite is the youngest pluton in the Yosemite Valley. It makes up much of the rock exposed at Glacier Point, the Royal Arches, and of course Half Dome itself. You cross this granite on the trail to Vernal and Nevada falls. The varying ages of these plutons suggest that major episodes of magma activity were separated by long periods with relatively little pluton formation.

Within these massive granitic bodies are smaller dikes or intrusions of rock that invaded the larger rock formations at a later date. One obvious dike formation is seen as a dark band on the southeastern face of El Capitan. Some imaginative viewers think it resembles a map of North America.

Outside of the Yosemite Valley, many similar granitic rocks are found. Granites near the eastern portion of the park are composed of four different plutons that have intruded upon one another, like successively smaller pots nested one inside the other. These represent successive waves of magma invasion. Each new intrusion differs slightly in chemical composition from previous ones.

The oldest of the four plutons, the Kuna Crest granodiorite, is named for the Kuna Crest, where it was first identified. It is about 91 million years in age. One crosses the Kuna Crest granodiorite along the Gaylor Lakes Trail, which begins north of Tioga Pass. The next oldest is the Half

Dome granodiorite, best seen near Olmsted Point along Tenaya Lake. Immediately east of Tenaya Lake one crosses from the Half Dome granodiorite to the Cathedral Peak granodiorite. Its namesake, Cathedral Peak, as well as much of the exposed granite in the Tuolumne Meadows area, is composed of this granitic rock. The last and most central of the four major plutons is the Johnson granite porphyry. It is exposed at Johnson Peak south of Tuolumne Meadows. This is the youngest exposed granite in the park. Geologists believe Johnson Peak represents the root of an ancient volcano.

Eventually pluton formation ceased, and erosion stripped away the volcanoes overlying what was to become the Sierra Nevada region, exposing the granite beneath. At the time this process was reversed, approximately 25 million years ago, the relief of the Yosemite region was only a few thousand feet. Isolated islands of the former metamorphic roof remained on top of the granite. The metamorphic rocks capping Mounts Dana and Gibbs are relicts from this time.

Late Cenozoic Volcanics

Between 20 million and 5 million years ago a belt of volcanoes forming the southern extension of the Cascade Range erupted and blanketed the region north of Yosemite with ash and lava. Evidence of these eruptions is visible in the rocks exposed at Sonora Pass and the Darnelles. A few of these flows reached the northern portion of Yosemite and poured lava and ash into the Tuolumne River canyon upstream from Hetch Hetchy Reservoir. In addition, small volcanic eruptions have occurred within Yosemite during relatively recent times. One of these lava flows solidified as columnar basalt joints along the Tuolumne River. Known as the Little Devils Postpile, this is a miniature example of its larger namesake by Mammoth Lakes.

Although major volcanoes north of Yosemite had ceased erupting by 5 million years ago, volcanic activity continued east of the park in the Mono Lake and Long Valley areas. The ten-mile-by-twenty-mile Long Valley Caldera is a remnant of a huge explosion that occurred 700,000 years ago. It spewed forth more than twenty-five hundred times the amount of ash pumped into the atmosphere by the eruption of Mount St. Helens in 1980. The Mono Craters between Mammoth Lakes and Mono Lake have erupted as recently as 600 years ago.

Recent Uplift

About 10 million years ago, the Sierra Nevada as we know it did not exist. Then a change in plate motion caused the range to rise along faults that define its eastern flank. Slowly at first, then more rapidly, the Sierra Nevada was uplifted. Most of the range's rise occurred during the last 2 million years. At present, Mount Dana along the eastern border of Yosemite is rising one and a half inches every hundred years—a tremendous rate of uplift. Though the rocks exposed in the Sierra Nevada are relatively old, the range itself is one of the youngest in the West.

Gold Deposits

One consequence of pluton development is mineralization. When molten rock cools, water is given off. This liquid contains high concentrations of metals that were present in minute amounts in the original molten rock. This supersaturated magma soup squeezes into cracks and fissures in the overlying rock and eventually cools and solidifies to form veins of mineral-bearing stone. Depending upon the temperature, original mixture of minerals in the concentrate, and other factors, these veins may contain gold, silver, lead, copper, and a variety of other minerals. When rivers strip away the overlying rocks, the mineral-rich veins appear, and gold and other metals wash into the rivers. The 1849 California gold rush was prompted by the discovery of this loose or placer gold in the foothills along the western margin of the Sierra Nevada.

Once placer deposits were exhausted, miners sought to discover Mother Lode veins that held the concentrated ore. Most gold-bearing veins occur in metamorphic rocks like those found in the foothills and along the eastern margin of Yosemite. Not surprisingly, miners explored some of the metavolcanic rocks along Yosemite's eastern border. Most evidence of this period is gone; however, an old miner's cabin can still be found near Mono Pass below Mount Lewis. And those traveling the Tioga Road follow a highway that was originally built to access mines near Saddlebag Lake just beyond the park's eastern border.

Recent Geological Influences

After the Sierra Nevada uplift began, three major influences shaped its present appearance—jointing, water erosion, and glaciation. Joints are cracks in bedrock thought to have been created by the stresses induced

This bedrock, layered along joints seen in the bottom of the photo, has been covered by glacial moraine, a mixture of unsorted dirt and rock. Glacial moraine is typically well drained and therefore prone to drought. The chaparral on top is adapted to warm, well-drained soils.

by uplift. Most joints in Yosemite are northeast- or northwest-trending. Parallel jointing patterns are obvious on granite slabs near the Olmsted Point pullout. Joints also create the ledges and handholds exploited by climbers scaling Yosemite's granite faces.

There are several kinds of jointing visible in Yosemite. Exfoliation is the term given to the process that produces the broad, onionlike layers common throughout the park. These are responsible for many named features, such as the Royal Arches. Because granites are formed under pressure, pressure is released as they are exposed by erosion. The rock then bows upward, and its outer layers gradually peel off in sheets from the underlying layers. This results in the smooth, rounded domes common in Yosemite. The bowed surfaces of Liberty Cap and Pywiack, Fairview,

Several rounded domes are visible in this view across Tenaya Lake toward 12,590-foot Mount Conness on the horizon. They were formed when overlaying rock was eroded, relieving pressure and permitting the bedrock to fracture and peel away. Domes are relatively rare in the world, and more are found in Yosemite than anywhere else.

This bedrock near Olmsted Point shows parallel fractures in the rock created by stresses associated with the uplift of the Sierra Nevada. Such joints control how cliffs and mountains are eroded and often determine stream location.

Half Dome is not, as is commonly thought, the remaining half of a dome partially removed by glaciers. Rather, weathering along joints has gradually eroded the rock, etching the dramatic face we see today.

Lembert, and Polly domes all result from the tendency of granitic rocks to exfoliate. Such domes are most abundant among granites with widely spaced or few joints.

Since joints are areas of weakness in otherwise nearly homogeneous granitic rock, they are exploited by weathering processes like water and frost. The resulting linear hollows have, in many cases, become stream channels.

The linear face of Half Dome, which appears to have been sliced off by a knife, is yet another example of jointing. It is not the result of glaciation, as many presume, although glaciers did remove some of the debris that had fallen from the cliff faces. Rather, Half Dome's rounded top is due to exfoliation. Rock faces peeled away from both sides of the dome, leaving vertical cliffs. The other "half" was never there.

Chemical composition of the bedrock influences jointing. For example, the nearly sheer face of El Capitan is the result of its lack of jointing, which in turn is due to the high quartz content of its granites. Thus the great cliff face of El Capitan is so sheer because its granite bedrock has few joints to assist weathering and erosion.

Lee Vining Canyon, which lies east of Yosemite National Park on the Inyo National Forest, was deepened and given its steep-sided, flat-bottomed appearance by the Lee Vining Glacier, which once flowed through it.

Erosion by Water and Glaciers

As the Sierra Nevada was uplifted, the gradients of streams flowing off the mountains increased, permitting greater erosion of the underlying rock. The deep canyons of the Tuolumne and Merced rivers were carved primarily by water during the past two million years. Although glaciers later occupied many of the upper tributaries and main river canyons, the lower sections were never glaciated. These canyons have retained the V shape characteristic of water-carved canyons.

About the same time as the Sierra Nevada uplift began in earnest some

Another glaciated valley is that of Tenaya Creek. In the foreground is North Dome and on the horizon, Unicorn Peak in the Cathedral Range.

two million years ago, the entire Northern Hemisphere was experiencing a major cooling trend. The climate over much of North America became slightly cooler, but more importantly, it became wetter as well. Increased precipitation permitted snow to accumulate to such an extent that the annual summer melting could not entirely eliminate the snowpack. Over time, this snow was metamorphosed into ice. As the ice grew thicker, it acquired plasticity and began to ooze like thick, cold toothpaste. This ice movement reshaped the landscape. In the Yosemite region it has been one of the greatest influences upon the outward physical characteristics of the land.

Glaciers sculpt the landscape in a variety of ways. Embedded in the ice are chunks of rocks and boulders plucked from the underlying bedrock. The tremendous weight of the ice, combined with the filing power of the embedded rock debris, makes a glacier a fine tool for smoothing obstructions. A moving glacier acts like a giant file that bevels surfaces. The bottoms of valleys are flattened, while the sides are steepened so that they take on a characteristic U-shaped appearance in cross section. The

Yosemite Valley was once occupied by a glacial lake, and today the flat valley floor is covered with lake sediment. El Capitan is on the left and Bridalveil Fall pours from the hanging valley on the right. Half Dome and Clouds Rest are partially visible in the center background.

Pine frames the U-shaped, glaciated upper portion of Tenaya Creek valley.

U-shaped valleys of the Lyell Fork of the Tuolumne, upper Virginia Creek, and even the Yosemite Valley reflect past glaciation.

Since tributary valleys have a smaller catchment basement, it is not surprising that they had smaller glaciers as well. These tributary glaciers flowed downstream to meet the main trunk valley glaciers, which were thicker and had greater erosive power. After the glaciers retreated, these side valleys were typically left stranded, hanging perched high above the main floor of the valley. Most of the waterfalls in the Yosemite Valley flow from tributary hanging valleys. Bridalveil Fall, for example, cascades over the lip of a hanging valley created by a glacier in the Bridalveil Creek drainage. Other falls issuing from hanging valleys include Yosemite, Ribbon, Illilouette, and Tueeulala.

Dirt and rocks in the bottom of a glacier act like sandpaper to grind away at bedrock, leaving behind glacial polish.

These percussion marks were created by rocks embedded in the base of a glacier as it moved over the bedrock. The gouges indicate the direction of glacier flow.

Deep U-shaped valleys are not the only marks left upon the land by glaciers. As the ice moves over the bedrock, the embedded boulders and rocks dig scratches or what are called glacial striations into the underlying rock surface. Because these scratches reveal the direction of the moving ice, it's possible to determine the source of glacial ice long after its passage. John Muir called these striations the "tracks of glaciers." Sometimes a glacier gouges half-moons in the bedrock; these are known as chatter marks. Like striations, they indicate the direction of travel. At times the grinding makes the underlying rock as smooth and slick as glass. This is called glacial polish.

When a glacier overrides a hill, it plucks rocks from the downstream side and smooths the uphill side. The resulting *roches moutonnées*, said to look like resting sheep, are common in the Tuolumne Meadows area. Liberty Cap, Pothole Dome, and Lembert Dome are classic examples.

Ice that forms in the hollows of peaks alternately freezes to the bedrock and moves downhill, pulling away pieces of the mountain with it. When this process is repeated the glacier gradually quarries out a steep-walled, bowl-shaped depression called a cirque. Many of the high peaks in Yosemite have glacial cirques along their sides.

The Merced Glacier passed over Liberty Cap and formed an elongated, rounded rock known as a roche moutonnée. *Nevada Falls was named because its cascades were like an "avalanche of snow."*

The steep-walled basin near the top of Mount Hoffman is an example of a glacial cirque, formed at the head of a glacier. The continual scooping and plucking of ice at the rock wall steepened it into a cliff.

This bowl-like basin, a perfect example of a glacially carved cirque lake, holds Vogelsang Lake in the Cathedral Range.

The unsorted mix of large and small boulders among a dirt matrix in this moraine near Dana Fork indicates glacial origins. Water-deposited rock would have been sorted by size.

If two or more glaciers carve opposite sides of a single ridge, they eventually produce a knife-edged crest or arête. If three sides are attacked by glaciers, you get a matterhorn, named for the famous Matterhorn in Europe. Matterhorn Peak and Cathedral Peak in Yosemite were both sculpted by glacial action.

Often the bowl-like depressions in cirque basins fill with water, creating what are known as cirque lakes. If the lakes are small, they are sometimes called tarns. Both cirque and tarn lakes are very common in the Yosemite high country. In fact, nearly all of the lakes in the park can be attributed to glacial action.

Rocks and dirt embedded in the sole of the glacier act like a giant rasp, grinding and polishing the bedrock beneath. The isolated boulders resting upon the bedrock are known as glacial erratics. They were carried in the glacial ice and deposited as the ice melted.

The small lakes in the Tioga Tarns area near Tioga Pass were formed when blocks of ice within the glacial moraine melted. The peak visible in the right skyline is 12,764-foot Mount Gibbs.

If average temperatures rise, precipitation declines, and ice melt exceeds the formation of new ice. When this happens a glacier begins to retreat. As it does so, it drops its load of ground up rock, boulders, and dirt, called glacial till. This till is easy to discern from water-sorted deposits because it typically contains rocks and dirt of all sizes and shapes mixed together, whereas waterborne materials are sorted by size and weight.

Glacial moraines are also composed of unsorted rock piles. *Moraine* is French for "hill" or "rubble heap." Unlike till, morainal deposits tend to reflect glacial shapes. Thus terminal moraines are frequently horseshoe-shaped, but lateral moraines, which form along the sides of glaciers,

Highway 120 now runs where the Lee Vining Glacier once covered the valley floor in the Inyo National Forest, east of Yosemite National Park. The glacier left behind lateral moraines, seen as the low forested hill on the left. The flat-topped peak on the center horizon is Mount Dana, second highest peak in Yosemite National Park.

appear as hills snaking in a linear fashion across the landscape. The low hills that enclose the lower portion of Lee Vining Canyon east of the Tioga Pass are lateral moraines from the Lee Vining Glacier. Moraines also occur in the Yosemite Valley; however, because these moraines are covered by vegetation, they are more difficult to discern. Nevertheless, one good place to see moraines is the jumbled pile of unsorted boulders on the hike to Mirror Lake along Tenaya Creek.

Sometimes ice becomes trapped in a moraine during a glacier's retreat. The melted ice later forms small lakes known as kettle ponds. Kettle ponds are quite common near Tioga Pass.

Glacial erratics are another common feature of glaciated landscapes. These are boulders or other rocks that appear to be out of place; they were transported by a glacier and left behind when the ice retreated. Erratics are common throughout the park; there are several good places to see them along the Tioga Road by Olmsted Point.

Although most of Yosemite's high country was covered with glacial ice during the height of the last major glacial advance, some peaks poked above the ice and remained unglaciated. The relatively flat surface plateau of Mount Dana is a classic example of unglaciated landscape. Although glaciers have carved cirques and bowls on Dana's flanks, the top was not touched by recent glaciation.

During the past million years, more than ten major glaciation events occurred in the Sierra Nevada. Evidence for previous glacial advances is relatively rare because more recent glaciation has destroyed most of the oldest deposits.

The most recent major glacial period, known locally as the Tioga Glaciation, reached its maximum extent fifteen thousand to twenty-thousand years ago and ended approximately ten thousand years ago.

During these glacial periods, ice fields up to four thousand feet thick covered much of the Sierran crest. Only the highest peaks, like Mount Dana and Mount Conness, stuck out above the surface. Long tributary glaciers flowed from the ice fields and filled pre-existing river valleys. The largest glacier flowed down the Tuolumne River canyon for sixty miles; it reached well beyond the present site of Hetch Hetchy Reservoir. Ice also occupied the Yosemite Valley as far as the Merced River gorge.

Although glaciers modified the features of the Yosemite Valley, much of the valley's present shape is the result of joint-controlled rockfall. Most of the debris was later removed by water. Recent research suggests that glaciation accounted for only 10 percent of the valley's widening and approximately 12 percent of the valley's excavation. This is considerably less than previously thought.

Nevertheless, past glaciation is responsible for Yosemite Valley's flat, level floor. A terminal moraine of the Merced Glacier blocked runoff as the ice melted, creating a lake in the valley that backed up water as far as Half Dome. Eventually sediments filled the lake, resulting in the present valley floor. Drillings show that bedrock by Glacier Point is covered by nearly two thousand feet of sediments.

Ice also moved down the steep canyons along the eastern escarpment of the range. The U-shaped canyon and moraines that mark the sides of Lee Vining Canyon are evidence of this glaciation. Runoff from the east-side glaciers flooded Lake Russell, the predecessor of Mono Lake, which was more than four hundred feet deeper and, consequently, much larger than today.

There are still a few relict glaciers left in Yosemite's high country. These glaciers owe their origins not to the last major ice age, but to a recent cooling trend that reached its maximum about 1850. Most of them barely flow anymore. Glaciers persist on Mount Lyell and Mount Maclure and on the north and east slopes of several peaks along the eastern border of the park, such as Mount Dana, Kuna Peak, Matterhorn Peak, and Mount Conness.

VEGETATION

With elevations ranging from 2,000 feet to 13,000 feet, it is not surprising that Yosemite has diverse plant communities. Many different microclimates are represented, ranging from hot, nearly desertlike conditions to treeless tundra that is not appreciably different from conditions in the Arctic.

The pronounced elevational difference creates numerous microhabitats that support more than fifteen hundred species of plants. It would be impossible to discuss each species. Instead I will discuss some of the major plant communities. These are typically defined by their major tree species because trees are easy to learn and a prominent feature of the Sierran landscape.

Characteristics of Mature Forests

The most notable feature of Yosemite is its forests. In many ways they rival the park's spectacular cliffs, waterfalls, and domes for attention. John Muir called the Sierran forests the "grandest and most beautiful in the world." I am certainly inclined to agree with his assessment. Like most people, I was at first taken by Yosemite's geological features, but what stays with me is not the images of Half Dome or El Capitan, spectacular though they may be, but the smell, feel, and look of the Sierran forests.

Part of their beauty lies in their diversity. There are eighteen species of conifers; many reach their greatest dimensions in this range. A special feature of these forests is the giant sequoia. This species is restricted to seventy-five groves in the Sierra; three of these occur in Yosemite National Park.

In forestry the typical woodlands of Yosemite are frequently referred to as overmature and decadent because many of the large, old trees no longer grow at their maximum rates. By this definition, the most decadent forests are those of giant sequoia; however, these are economic rather than biological terms. Whether a tree is maximizing wood fiber accumulation is not of much consequence to the forest. Furthermore, from an ecological perspective, an overmature forest has features not found in younger forests.

Large trees, with their big branches, provide shelter from wind, rain, and heat to species like the spotted owl. Older forests also contain abundant snags, which are important for many cavity-nesting birds, as well as squirrels and other small mammals.

When the large boles fall to the ground they provide hiding cover for small mammals, reptiles, and other wildlife on the forest floor. If these trees fall into streams, they provide habitat for aquatic insects and fishes. Since large trees rot more slowly than small trees, they are also a source of nutrients that can be stored and released over the long term.

Finally, once the trees rot sufficiently, animals can dig out the decaying wood to make warm, secure dens. Marten in Wyoming have been shown to require such pulpy logs in order to survive occasional cold snaps.

Large decaying logs also act as sponges, soaking up water in the winter. Young seedlings that happen to tap into these water storage tanks can survive the Sierra's summer drought. Furthermore, except in the driest summers these wet logs act as firebreaks and help to discourage the spread of fires.

Even in the days before modern forestry came to the Sierra, not all forests were older mature trees. Fires burned some of the woodlands each summer. In spite of such natural disturbances within the park, the managed forests outside of Yosemite have younger trees and are far more fragmented than the park's forests.

Historical Changes in Park Vegetation

Concentrated use, particularly in the Yosemite Valley, as well as historic uses that degraded or destroyed natural ecological processes have brought about significant changes in the park's vegetation. Old photographs suggest that Yosemite Valley was once more open and swampy, with far more black oak and fewer thickets of pine, incense cedar, and white fir. It is, for example, estimated that 90 percent of the black oak woodlands in the valley are now gone. There are a number of factors responsible for this vegetation change. One is fire suppression. This will be discussed in more detail below. In general, frequent fires, some of which were set by Indians, tended to kill young trees, maintain meadows, and favor species like black

The 90-percent decline of black oak in Yosemite is due in part to fire suppression. The loss of oak, an important food source for everything from acorn woodpeckers to black bears, has serious consequences for the park's wildlife.

oak that can sprout from the root crown should a fire destroy the trunk.

A second factor is the extensive domestic livestock grazing that once took place in the valley. In the early years of the park, many horses, the major source of transportation, were pastured in the valley. In addition, since fresh milk was difficult to obtain prior to refrigeration, cows were also allowed to graze in the valley. As a result, much of the valley floor was once fenced. Trampling by livestock compacted soils in the pastures, and selective grazing on some plants permitted the invasion or expansion of less desirable species. Many non-native weeds were spread throughout the valley in the feces of domestic animals, and some exotics like Kentucky bluegrass were planted to provide hay for domestic livestock. Valley meadows continued to be grazed until the 1930s.

Some of the valley meadows were even plowed. In the 1880s Leidig Meadow was planted three times to wheat and hay. Ahwahnee and Stoneman meadows were also cultivated.

As a result of these disturbances, the National Park Service estimates that the Yosemite Valley meadows have declined by 59 percent, from a total of 820 acres in 1868 to 339 acres by 1990.

Efforts to drain swampy ground also modified the valley. A high water table was once maintained by a terminal moraine that crossed the valley near El Capitan. Upstream, the Merced River meandered across the valley in a braided fashion; today it is a single channel. In 1879, Galen Clark, the first guardian of Yosemite, dynamited boulders to remove the terminal moraine that dammed the river. This lowered the downstream end of the river and increased stream gradient and velocity, which in turn caused increased erosion and channel downcutting.

In response to the increased erosion, riprap was placed in the Merced River; however, this only accelerated the water's movement downstream and exacerbated the erosion. Bridges that were constructed also changed stream flow by constricting the channel and accelerating downcutting.

Erosion was made even worse by the practice of removing logjams and woody debris that otherwise would have slowed the river current and stabilized streambanks. This practice began in 1882 and continued until 1989. Woody debris not only slows erosion, it also provides habitat for fishes and aquatic insects. Fish populations have dramatically declined in the Merced River because of these and other alterations that have compromised the structure and stability of its streambanks. As a result of all these modifications in the landscape, species like incense cedar, Douglas-fir, canyon live oak, California bay, and white fir have increased in num-

Note how trees are banded along the base of Mammoth Peak. Trees do not grow in the meadow because conditions are too cold and moisture levels excessive.

bers and distribution, while black oak, ponderosa pine, black cotton-wood, white alder, and willow have declined.

It may be impossible to restore the valley to its original condition, but efforts are under way to reverse the effects of some unwise past decisions, or at the least to minimize their future impacts.

Influence of Microclimate on Plant Distribution

Where a plant grows is determined by the interaction of many factors including moisture, topography, soil type, wind, fire, and influences of humans and animals. Exposure to the sun, or aspect, greatly influences plant distribution. South-facing slopes are relatively dry; north-facing slopes at the same elevation are cooler and more moist. This difference in microclimate is particularly noticeable in the Yosemite Valley. Flowers often bloom on the north side (which faces south) of the valley in February and March, while snow still cloaks the north-facing south slope just a mile away.

Cold air drainage also influences plant distribution. Because cold air settles in valley bottoms, at times valleys are as much as twenty degrees colder than adjacent slopes and knolls that are a few hundred feet higher. Cold air drainage can cause frost damage to tree saplings; this allows meadows to be maintained in basins of the subalpine forests.

All other things being equal, moisture increases with elevation, while temperature decreases. Marked changes in vegetation track these differences in microclimate. The transitions between plant communities are seldom sharp or well defined; rather plant species fall out along a continuum or gradient. Nevertheless, some general patterns are obvious.

One of the dominant characteristics of the Sierra Nevada is summer drought. Drought gives conifers a competitive advantage. Evergreen needles lose less water than deciduous leaves. Furthermore, since soil moisture rapidly declines in the summer, Sierran trees need to be ready to photosynthesize when moisture subsequently becomes available during the fall, winter, and spring. Evergreen needles allow conifers to photosynthesize whenever temperatures rise above freezing, permitting them to take advantage of soil moisture during seasons when deciduous species are leafless. Sierran deciduous trees are found only where soil moisture or surface moisture is high, such as near seeps, riparian areas along rivers or streams, or springs.

*Prior to active fire suppression, many Sierran forests were open and park-like.
Fire suppression has permitted shade-tolerant species like white fir to invade,
increasing fuel loading and fire danger and reducing habitat for species like the
ponderosa pine. The controlled burn used to kill this young fir permitted
mature trees like the pine in the center to survive.*

Fire Ecology

Summer drought is also responsible for the prominent role of fire in
Sierran ecosystems. The greatest force shaping mid-elevation forests has
been fire. Prior to the fire suppression policies begun a hundred years ago,
Sierran forests were typically open and parklike because of frequent, low-
intensity blazes. On occasion large fires swept across hundreds of thousands of acres; however, most fires were local and small. As a rule, they
burned only the understory litter, grasses, shrubs, and smaller trees, and
left the mature trees alive. These "cool" fires occurred as often as every

five to ten years in some of the drier, lower forests. The resulting forests were characterized by large, widely spaced trees growing in open stands with little understory.

John Muir described this enchanting quality in his book *The Mountains of California*. "The inviting openness of the Sierra woods is one of their most distinguishing characteristics. The trees of all the species stand more or less apart in groves, or in small, irregular groups, enabling one to find a way nearly everywhere, along sunny colonnades and through openings that have a smooth, park-like surface. . . . One would experience but little difficulty in riding horseback through the successive belts all the way up to the storm-beaten fringes of the icy peaks."

Lafayette Bunnell, one of the members of the Mariposa Battalion that saw Yosemite in 1851, later recalled that "the valley at the time of discovery presented the appearance of a well-kept park. . . . There was then but little undergrowth in the park-like valley, and a half day's work in lopping off branches . . . enabled us to speed our horses uninterrupted through the groves."

Open forests such as the ones Muir and Bunnell described are rare today. This is largely because of fire suppression, which has permitted dense stands of trees to replace the once open forests. Although it seems contrary to common sense, fires are to the Sierran forest what rain is to the tropical rainforest, a natural ecological process upon which the entire forest ecosystem depends.

Yet because of our bias that labels any blaze as bad, few visitors realize that the healthiest forest stands in the park are those that have recently experienced a fire. The blackened snags and partially burned trees represent ecological health. Despite propaganda and uninformed journalism to the contrary, fires don't necessarily destroy a forest; but the absence of fire can.

Unlike eastern deciduous forests, where moisture is available throughout the year, Sierran forests experience dry summers with low humidity and high air temperatures. These conditions are conducive to fires but not to biological decomposition by bacteria and fungi. In the moist environment of the eastern United States, most leaves, needles, and even entire logs molder, or disintegrate, quickly, and nutrients are rapidly returned to the soil. In the arid West, however, little decomposition takes place during the summer drought. When it's warm enough for bacteria and fungi to become active, it's usually too dry. As a consequence, litter and logs break down very slowly. Instead, fire allows nutrients bound up in dead litter to be released and washed into the soil and streams.

Fires also cleanse a forest. The heat of a blaze kills forest pathogens including wood-boring insects. Even smoke has been shown to reduce the vigor of or kill some arboreal forest pathogens.

Because fires typically do not kill all trees in a stand, the trees that survive a blaze are freed of competition. Consequently they have more light, water, and nutrients available. This enables them to better resist disease, insects, and drought. The recent die-offs in many Sierran forests, such as those around Lake Tahoe, are frequently attributed to insects or diseases; however, the vulnerability of these trees to such natural agents may result from crowding due to the absence of fire.

Periodic fires also prevent trees from invading meadows. Many of the lower-elevation meadows in Yosemite have suffered from tree encroachment in the absence of fires.

Fires create snags. Cavities carved in snags are home to more than a quarter of the Sierran bird species including woodpeckers, nuthatches, and owls, as well as some mammals, such as flying squirrels and bats. Snags that fall into streams provide fish habitat as well.

Fires create ideal conditions for seed germination and seedling survival, because competing vegetation is removed. This frees up water and other nutrients for young trees and other plants. In addition, many tree seeds require for successful germination the bare mineral soil that is exposed after a forest fire.

Unfortunately one consequence of one hundred years of fire suppression has been a change from low-intensity, "cool" fires to high-intensity crown fires termed stand replacement blazes. As a result the root systems and root crowns of species that normally sprout after a cooler burn are damaged. There is no good way to reduce fuel buildup without fires.

Nevertheless, it would be wrong to conclude that all hot fires are unnatural. Even before there was significant fire suppression, forests at higher elevations experienced fewer fires because of the shorter fire season. The longer interval between blazes allowed greater accumulations of fuels. These areas often experienced stand replacement burns.

Although fires were very common at the lower and middle elevations of the Sierra, they were relatively rare above 9,000 feet elevation in the

Ponderosa pine is a fire-adapted species. The thick bark helps protect the pine from low-intensity surface burns. (Note the fire scar at the base of the trunk.) The lack of lower branches prevents fires from "laddering" or jumping up into the crown.

The black oak not only survives fires by sprouting from roots after its above-ground parts are burned, but it actually depends upon fires to kill off pine and other species that would otherwise overtake the site, shading out young black oaks.

sparsely forested subalpine and alpine areas. This is partly because of the lack of fuel. Many of the subalpine basins are characterized by large areas of bare rock interspersed with wet meadows and lakes. These acted as natural fire breaks, keeping most fires local and small. In addition, the low productivity of such sites limits the accumulation of fuels. As a consequence, suppression activities probably have not greatly influenced the overall fire regime at the higher elevations of the park.

If fires are a normal and natural part of the environment, then we would expect many plants to be adapted to or at least tolerant of fire, and indeed, this is the case.

Many of the Sierran tree species have characteristics that permit them to survive low-intensity burns. For instance, ponderosa pine, Jeffrey pine, incense cedar, Douglas-fir, red fir, and giant sequoia all have thick bark that resists flames. The bark of some of the larger sequoias may be nearly two feet thick.

In addition, most of these trees are self-pruning; they lose their lower branches as they grow older. This makes it more difficult for a ground fire to climb into the crown by the way of the lower branches.

Some species sprout from root crowns after a fire has killed or burned off the aboveground parts. Black oak is a root sprouter, as is aspen. Aspen sends up thousands of root suckers per acre after its aboveground parts have been destroyed.

The cones of some species require heat in order to open and release their seeds. Lodgepole pine and sequoia share this characteristic.

Although many species can tolerate fire, some cannot. White fir is very susceptible to flames. It has very thin bark, coupled with branches that sweep down to the ground. Where fires are frequent, there are few mature white firs.

Fire suppression in the Sierra began with the first white settlers. It has continued without critical scrutiny almost until the present. Even today, we are bombarded with anti-fire propaganda, in particular, from the U.S. Forest Service. Posters display wide-eyed deer and other wildlife fleeing for their lives in front of a blaze. This misrepresents what really happens. Most animals simply walk away from a fire. Nevertheless, so strong is the bias against fires, we can't even discuss it without using value-laden words. How many times have we read or heard about how a fire "destroyed" so many acres of forest or fire fighters "battled" the blaze as if it were an enemy? Yet, from an ecological perspective, fire merely changes the forest, and from the forest's perspective the real enemies are the fire fighters who attempt to put out a naturally started fire.

Some people early on recognized the important ecological role that fires have played in the Sierran forests. William H. Mills, a member of the state commission set up to guide management of the Yosemite Valley and Mariposa Grove State Park, warned in 1889 that litter accumulating in the big trees "was endangering the forest." In providing evidence for his statements, Mills noted, "You can see the evidence for past burning through this forest. Many of [the trees] are blackened and burned at the roots."

But it was not until the 1960s that managers began to seriously question fire suppression policies. The lack of regeneration among sequoias provided the motivation. Studies of the giant trees showed that moderate

The Merced River reflects the majestic Half Dome.

Dogwood along Tenaya Creek shows its autumn colors.

A backpacker on Horse Ridge above Hart Lake views Clark Range.

Yosemite is well known for its geological wonders, including the Sierra Nevada Range. Shown here is Kuna Peak.

Bigleaf maple surrounds the John Muir Trail.

El Capitan rises from the waters of the Merced River.

At the summit of Mount Hoffman, climbers find this view of Tuolumne Peak.

The sun sets on Half Dome as seen from Glacier Point.

El Capitan provides an imposing background to
the beauty of the Merced River.

*Red paintbrush accents
the greenery near
Reymann Lake.*

*Pinnacles above Nelson
Lake display their alpenglow
at sunrise and sunset.*

Pine needles and bigleaf maple leaves carpet the floor of Yosemite Valley.

A black oak, framed by Half Dome, shows its fall foliage.

Incense cedar looms at the edge of Tenaya Creek.

The dry bed of Lewis Creek leads toward Clark Range.

The magnificent sequoia can live for thousands of years.

A spot on
Virginia Creek
provides this
view of Shepherd
Peak and Crest.

The leaves of the bigleaf maple are
six to twelve inches across.

Yosemite Falls is one of the ten highest waterfalls in the world.

A sequoia can grow to three hundred feet and attain a diameter of thirty feet.

burning was essential for sequoia seed germination and seedling survival. This led to a closer look at the processes that had previously shaped Sierran forests.

In keeping with its policy of preserving natural ecological processes, the National Park Service has implemented a "prescribed natural fire" policy. Fires are permitted to burn in most wilderness areas of the park as long as they meet predetermined conditions. Such fires must not pose a threat to human life or property and there must be acceptable fuel loadings and defensible boundaries. Since 1972 when the prescribed natural fire program began in Yosemite, 424 fires have burned 49,000 acres under this policy.

In areas where prescribed natural fire parameters can't be met, such as the Yosemite Valley, agency personnel have embarked on fire restoration. Under this "prescribed fire or controlled burn" program, blazes are purposely ignited under very strict conditions. Controlled burns usually take place in early spring while the ground is still relatively wet; they aim to reduce fuel accumulations and restore fire's role in the valley at a time when the likelihood of a major blaze is limited. Since 1970 more than 28,333 acres have been treated by this method.

In August 1990, lightning ignited more than twenty-five fires on the western flank of Yosemite. By the time the flames had died, more than 13,000 acres of Yosemite had burned. The park was closed for eleven days. Sixty-eight cabins in Foresta were destroyed. To many the fires were a disaster; however, the real disaster was not the blaze but the amount of money spent attempting to control the uncontrollable.

Many studies, including those following the Yellowstone fires, have shown that when conditions are ripe for a blaze, almost no amount of fire fighting can halt the sweep of flames. In nearly all instances, fires are finally controlled not because of human efforts, but as a consequence of changing fire conditions—usually rain or other precipitation. In essence, we are merely flailing at the flames so we have the appearance of doing something.

Furthermore, suppression in one year just means there will be that much more fuel available to support an even larger blaze in future years. It's like borrowing money to pay for things you can't afford. Sooner or later you have to pay off the debt. In the Sierra, it's not a question of if the forest will burn, but when.

This is not to suggest that we should allow fire to burn up every home or building that may lie in its path. But it is much more cost effective and less dangerous to defend buildings than to try to stop a blaze on all fronts. One can argue, however, that constructing a home in fire-dependent forests like those of the Sierra is analogous to putting your house in the middle of the hundred-year floodplain. One can't predict exactly when the river will overrun its banks, but it's certain that if you build in an inappropriate place, you will suffer the consequences.

Plant Communities of Yosemite

As one ascends the Sierra Nevada from its foothills to the alpine zone, one crosses both temperature and moisture gradients. Patterns of plant distribution emerge. These are by no means abrupt; nevertheless, they do occur in a predictable order.

Although this book describes discrete zones in which the dominant plants differ, patterns are not always so neat and ordered on the ground. Thus, though I discuss red fir as if it were typically found separate from white fir, the truth is that both species are often found mixed together. The same thing could be said for numerous other combinations of species.

Foothills

The foothill zone lies between 500 and 4,000 feet. Because the lowest elevation in the park is approximately 2,000 feet, however, the foothills plant communities make up a relatively small portion of Yosemite. But in order to approach the park, it is necessary to pass through the foothills communities described below.

The Sierra foothills receive between fifteen and thirty-five inches of precipitation annually; the higher precipitation occurs at the upper elevations. Nearly all of it falls in the winter. Summer temperatures are warm—often approaching one hundred degrees in some of the canyon bottoms such as along the lower Merced River gorge. South-facing slopes experience especially hot temperatures and drought conditions.

The effects of heat are more pronounced because almost no precipitation occurs during the warm months of late spring through early fall. Most water is available in winter and early spring; therefore plant growth occurs during this season, rather than in summer. Many plants from this zone go into summer dormancy to avoid the season of greatest stress.

Small leaves with a thick, waxy cuticle that reduces water losses are another adaptation for dealing with drought and heat. Some species, like manzanita, orient their lives vertically to reduce the surface area exposed to the heat of the sun.

The vegetation of the foothill zone can be broken down further into grasslands, chaparral, riparian woodlands, and blue oak–pine savanna.

GRASSLANDS

These are found at the lowest elevations, on dry, south-facing slopes, and some woodlands understories. Most of the native perennial grasses of this zone were eliminated by overgrazing. Now most species are annuals introduced from Europe, like wild oat, red brome, and foxtail fescue. Common wildflowers associated with these grasslands include buttercup, larkspur, brodiaea, meadow form, tidy tips, lupine, California poppy, Indian pink, fiddleneck, madia, and baby blue-eyes.

Grasses are well adapted to fire. Buried in soil, the seeds of annual grasses survive the heat of a fire and sprout the following spring after the winter rains. Perennial grasses sprout from their root crowns.

CHAPARRAL

These thickets consist of dense shrubs typically less than twelve feet high that cover the drier slopes, particularly those with shallow, well-drained soils. *Chaparral* comes from the Spanish word for "scrub oak." Most chaparral in Yosemite comprises several species of manzanita, such as whiteleaf manzanita, as well as whitethorn, buckbrush, deerbrush, and mountain mahogany, and shrub oaks like canyon oak, sometimes called canyon live oak. Canyon oak is common on the south-facing slopes in the Yosemite Valley; for instance, it can be seen west of El Capitan. You also pass through a great deal of chaparral on the Big Oak Flat Road once it begins to descend into the valley. The best developed canyon oak chaparral is found in tributary canyons of the Merced River.

Although very rare in the Sierra, knobcone pine, is occasionally found mixed in with the various shrub oaks and chaparral. In the Yosemite area it is found along the Merced River near El Portal and along the Old Colterville Road above Big Meadow.

Many chaparral species produce toxins that inhibit the growth of competing shrubs and sometimes even their own seedlings. Known as allelopathy, this phenomenon ensures sufficient moisture and nutrients for the existing plants.

Like grasses, chaparral species are adapted to fire. First of all, they mature and produce seeds at an early age. These seeds tend to be fire-resistant. Second, some species, such as manzanita and some members of the genus ceanothus, require heat from a fire to crack the tough, outer

Manzanita, a common chaparral shrub, has small thick leaves that reduce water loss, an adaptation to drought and heat. It also sprouts from its roots if the top of the shrub is removed, an adaptation to recovery after fire. Fire was once a common feature of the manzanita habitat.

seed coat prior to germination. Finally, nearly all chaparral species are crown or root sprouters; that is, after a fire the roots send forth new plants. Because these plants already have established root systems to gather soil moisture, they grow rapidly and outcompete other plants attempting to establish themselves on the dry, hot slopes. Common chaparral root sprouters include canyon oak, toyon, manzanita, and chamise.

Many chaparral species even contain volatile oils that make them more flammable. This ensures that they will burn. Fires in this type of vegetation tend to be very hot; they often wipe out any competing trees, thereby ensuring that chaparral vegetation will continue to dominate a site. The average interval between fires in the chaparral zone is ten to forty years.

Fires increase soil fertility in several ways. The addition of ash returns nutrients to the soil. Furthermore, the bare soil, increased sunlight, and rich nutrients released by combustion encourage the establishment of nitrogen-fixing plants like lupine and ceanothus. To summarize, fires set back succession but do little harm to the chaparral community.

RIPARIAN WOODLANDS

Riparian areas are the lush, thin, green lines of vegetation bordering rivers or streams. They occur along the South Forks of the Merced and Tuolumne rivers, plus along many of the smaller tributary streams. Riparian zones have abundant water close to the surface; hence, trees and shrubs of this zone do not display adaptations to drought. Many riparian species can also be found in places in the forests where seeps or springs create saturated soils. Typical riparian vegetation consists of various willow species, black cottonwood, California sycamore, and white alder. Bigleaf maple, and Pacific dogwood are also common associates. The dogwood, with its large, white blossoms, is particularly attractive in spring. Most of these riparian trees are winter deciduous, turning beautiful colors of gold and red in the autumn and remaining bare in the winter.

BLUE OAK–PINE SAVANNA

If you climb up out of the riparian zone to elevations between 2,000 and 4,000 feet, you'll encounter pine savannas with blue oak that have grassy understories. The best place to see this community within Yosemite is by the El Portal entrance.

These savannas are dominated by deciduous blue oak. Evergreen interior live oak and digger pine grow in slightly wetter sites. The *digger pine,* with its long, gray-green, lacy needles, eight- to twelve-inch cones, and open crown is easy to spot.

Blue oak is common on steep, dry slopes with shallow soils. Its large root system taps deep water sources, permitting it to survive the intense summer droughts that characterize this zone. Its oblong, shallow-lobed leaves and blue-green color distinguish it from other oaks.

Sometimes the spring-blooming *redbud,* named for the pink blossoms that appear before its leaves, is mixed in with these species at higher elevations. *California buckeye* is another common associate. In spring this tree has beautiful, large, white blossoms that set it apart from other trees. As an adaptation to drought, the buckeye loses its leaves by midsummer but retains its large, hanging, pearlike seed pods.

Mixed Coniferous Forests

The mixed coniferous forests can be broken down into two subzones. Transition forests dominated by black oak, ponderosa pine, incense cedar, sugar pine, and Douglas-fir are found between 4,000 and 6,000 feet. They grade into mid-elevation coniferous forests lying between 6,000 and 8,000 feet, the zone of greatest precipitation. Here grow giant sequoia, white fir, sugar pine, and Jeffrey pine.

TRANSITION FORESTS

The Yosemite Valley offers one of the best places to view transition forests. Large, yellow-barked ponderosa pines are scattered about the valley. Mixed in among the pines are the rust-colored trunks of incense cedars and scattered groves of the deciduous black oak. The large, dark green oak leaves, which turn golden in the autumn, add much to the beauty of the valley floor. Douglas-fir is found in moister locations, generally against the north-facing cliff faces or in side canyons like those on the trail to Nevada Falls.

In the past this zone was heavily influenced by frequent low-intensity fires—both natural and human-caused blazes. The average interval was eight to twelve years between fires. A hundred years of fire suppression, unfortunately, have permitted fuels to build to dangerous levels, and most

A ponderosa pine, its trunk blackened by a recent fire, frames Sentinel Rock in the Yosemite Valley.

fires today tend to be hotter and larger as nature attempts to correct the imbalances caused by past policies.

Black oak is the largest mountain oak; its trunks sometimes achieve widths of three feet or more. One tree in Yosemite measured thirty-six feet in girth. Its large, eight- to twelve-inch-long, deciduous leaves armed with pointed bristles make this tree a distinctive feature of the valley.

The Indians who lived in the Yosemite Valley were dependent upon black oak acorns as a dietary staple. Each family consumed as much as five hundred pounds of acorns a year. To ensure abundant acorn crops, the Indians set fire to meadows; this favored food-producing trees like the acorn-bearing black oak. Black oaks are well adapted to fire because they can sprout new shoots from their roots after fire.

Unfortunately, fire suppression has dramatically reduced black oak woodlands in the Yosemite Valley. According to research by the National Park Service, stands of black oak have declined by 90 percent in historical times. Grazing by domestic livestock in the early part of the century no doubt also had an impact. Today only four stands of black oak, totaling 143 acres, remain in the valley. However, the 1990 Arch Rock fire, which spread across much of the western portion of the park, stimulated many black oaks to sprout. A good place to see black oak sprouts is the burns located along the Big Oak Flat Road.

Fire suppression is not the only problem encountered by black oak, however. In high use areas, seedlings are trampled by people and eaten by deer and gophers. In an effort to restore the black oak woodlands that were formerly so characteristic of the valley, the National Park Service recently launched an oak restoration program. Oak seedlings were planted in fenced areas to control human trampling. In addition, protective netting below and above ground discourages browsing by deer and gophers.

Prior to fire suppression **ponderosa pine** forests were typically parklike and open with large boles that gave the appearance of columns. Next to digger pine, ponderosa pine is the most drought resistant of the west slope pines; therefore, it tends to be found in the transition from oak woodland to coniferous forest.

One adaptation of ponderosa pine to its dry habitat is an extensive root system. A study of seedlings found that young trees only three inches high had two-foot-long roots. The roots of a foot-tall tree might tap water

A tall straight bole and outstretched upper branches characterize the sugar pine. A popular timber species, mature sugar pines like this are largely gone from areas outside of the park.

supplies five feet below the surface. A sun-loving tree, ponderosa pine is gradually replaced by more shade-tolerant species like white fir and Douglas-fir if nothing interrupts normal succession. Nevertheless, an old ponderosa pine may exceed six hundred years of age and attain a girth of six feet or more.

Although ponderosa pine once dominated Yosemite Valley, *incense cedar* now outnumbers it. This is due to several factors. One is the ability of incense cedar to tolerate shade. In addition, fire suppression has allowed understory thickets of pine, cedar, and other species to develop. The resulting competition for water, nutrients, and light reduces the overall vitality of mature pines and makes them more vulnerable to insect attack and disease.

The large dissected leaves of the bigleaf maple gild the forest in autumn. A northern species that reaches its southern limits in the Sierra Nevada, the bigleaf maple occupies shady, cool sites.

The incense cedar, with its lacy foliage and cinnamon red bark, is sometime mistaken for a young sequoia. Like ponderosa pine, incense cedar has thick bark that helps it to survive periodic blazes.

Douglas-fir has soft, single needles about one inch long and thick, corky bark that protects mature trees from light, "cool" blazes. The best way to identify this species is by the three-pronged bracts of its cones. It is found in moist habitats in the park but reaches the southern limit of its distribution in the Sierra in the San Joaquin River drainage twenty miles south of Yosemite. Two large Douglas-firs beneath Half Dome by Mirror Lake stand two hundred feet tall and measure more than seven feet thick.

John Muir called the **sugar pine** "the noblest pine yet discovered, surpassing all others not merely in size but also in kingly beauty and majesty." This was once the primary timber species in the Sierra. Sadly, as a result of selective logging, large specimens are now relatively rare outside of preserves like Yosemite.

The sugar pine seldom forms pure stands. It usually grows mixed in with other conifers; nevertheless, this stately tree is easy to pick out even at a distance. On older trees, the tall, straight bole is branchless for a hundred feet above the ground; above this height it is crowned by limbs bearing eleven- to eighteen-inch-long cones that hang like Christmas ornaments. A large sugar pine may exceed two hundred feet in height and have a girth of ten feet.

In the moist side canyons and along streams in the transition forest one encounters the **bigleaf maple**, a deciduous tree with palm-shaped leaves six to twelve inches across. The huge leaves of this species turn golden in the autumn, adding much color to the otherwise somber coniferous forests it is typically associated with. This species reaches its southern limits in the Sierra.

The bigleaf maple's smaller cousin, the **mountain maple,** also grows in Yosemite. This multistemmed shrub seldom grows taller than twenty feet. Its leaves, much smaller than those of the bigleaf maple, also turn golden in autumn.

If you visit Yosemite in May, you might be fortunate enough to catch the **Pacific dogwood** in bloom. Its white blossoms measure up to six inches across and shine like Christmas decorations among the dark foliage of the coniferous forests. This species is well adapted to understory conditions. It is able to photosynthesize in only one-third of full sunlight and seldom grows more than thirty feet tall. It is common in the understories of western slope pine and sequoia forests between 3,000 and 6,000 feet elevation. Other understory plants of this zone include mountain misery, thimbleberry, gooseberry, wild rose, snowberry, greenleaf manzanita, deerbrush, and bracken fern.

MID-ELEVATION FORESTS

As one climbs higher in the Sierra, deep snowpacks provide a more predictable moisture source during the summer growing season. Cold

White fir, a shade-tolerant tree that now thrives throughout the Sierra Nevada because of fire suppression, has light-colored bark and needles two to three inches long.

temperatures and moist conditions favor species like sequoia, Jeffrey pine, white fir, and western white pine.

At higher elevations *Jeffrey pine* tends to replace ponderosa, which it resembles. Some speculate that Jeffrey pine tolerates colder temperatures. Both pines have scaly yellow-red bark and needles in bundles of three. The easiest way to tell the two apart is by the cones. Those of Jeffrey pine are typically five to eight inches long with prickles on the ends of scales that turn inward; ponderosa cones are two to five inches long and have prickles that point outward.

A tree that is increasingly prevalent in the understory of the pine forests as a result of fire suppression is the *white fir*. This species has two-inch-long, single needles and two- to five-inch-long cones that crowd the top third of the tree. Like all firs, the cones stand upright. The bark is silver-gray and smooth unless the tree is very large. White fir is partial to moist areas where annual precipitation is forty to sixty inches. On suit-able sites, it may comprise up to 80 percent of the trees, although it seldom forms pure stands. Fir is shade-tolerant, so it can grow beneath other species. Consequently, fir forests have a multi-layered appearance, with young and old trees mixed together. Unlike many other conifers, white fir has no adaptations to fire. Its branches sweep down to the ground, providing a ladder that rapidly carries flames into the crown.

The most memorable tree of the mixed coniferous forest is the massive, cinnamon-barked giant *sequoia*. Only seventy-five groves of these im-pressive trees are found in the entire world—all on the western slope of the Sierra. Their combined area equals only 35,000 acres. Three of these groves—the Tuolumne, Merced, and Mariposa—are found in Yosemite National Park.

Sequoia groves are restricted to moist, deep soils on ridges between 5,000 and 8,500 feet. Their confinement to ridges is sometimes attributed to past glaciation; it is thought that glaciers wiped out the sequoias in valley bottoms.

At one time sequoias were widespread in the mixed coniferous forests of both North America and Europe. As the climate turned colder and drier, the range of the sequoia gradually shrank. Today, it is found only in places where there is reliable summer moisture.

The sequoia lives for thousands of years and attains immense propor-tions. The oldest known individual is thirty-three hundred years old; the largest specimens exceed 300 feet in height and 30 feet in diameter. The

The Grizzly Giant in the Mariposa Sequoia Grove dwarfs human visitors.
Sequoias are relatively rare, found in only seventy-five groves along a
two-hundred-mile belt of the western Sierra Nevada. Yosemite is home to
three groves: the Tuolumne, Merced, and the largest group, the Mariposa.

General Grant Tree in Kings Canyon National Park measures 40.3 feet across its base and is 267.4 feet tall. The Grizzly Giant in Yosemite's Mariposa Grove is 30.7 feet in diameter at its base and still 16 feet in diameter 60 feet off the ground. Even its branches are enormous; the largest is 6 feet in diameter.

The sequoia's longevity is attributed to a number of factors. Its bark, often more than two feet thick, is resistant to disease, insects, and fire. Since the bark also contains no flammable oils, it is extremely fireproof. Even if a blaze should burn into the trunk, the tree has the ability to continue living in spite of the scar. The most common cause of mortality is toppling, to which sequoias are susceptible because of their shallow root systems.

Because they have extremely tiny seeds, sequoias require bare mineral soil for successful establishment. Fires are the primary means of creating the proper seed bed. Sequoia cones also tend to remain closed until heated. Thus fires prepare a suitable seed bed and also ensure an abundant seed crop.

The long-horned beetle assists seed dissemination by tunneling into sequoia cones. This causes them to dry out, open, and shed their seeds.

Flowers common throughout this mixed-conifer zone, either in the understory or in the small meadows that are common at this elevation, include Mariposa lily, blue penstemon, Harlequin lupine, meadow goldenrod, yarrow, harvest brodiaea, prince's pine, sneezeweed, cow parsnip, showy milkweed, pinedrop, canchalagua, Sierra lessingia, bleeding heart, and wild ginger. Flowering shrubs include elderberry, mock orange or syringa, western azalea, yerba santa, and spice bush.

Subalpine Communities

SUBALPINE FORESTS

The subalpine zone lies between 8,000 and 10,000 feet, the belt of greatest snowfall. You have to leave the Yosemite Valley to encounter it.

A distinctive characteristic of fir trees is that their cones grow erect and upright on the branches, as seen on this red fir, rather than drooping, as on most conifers. Fir cones disintegrate on the trees; they are seldom found on the ground.

Stands of red fir, among the most beautiful of the Sierran trees, are known as snow forests. They have adapted for growth at the elevation of greatest snowfall; their tight, narrow crowns allow them to shed the heavy snow.

Lodgepole pine is a subalpine species that grows in nearly pure stands on sites that are dry, rocky, or very wet. It is the only Sierran pine that has two needles to a bract.

Subalpine forests can be seen along the Glacier Point Road, but the best developed examples lie along the Tioga Road.

Characteristic species of the subalpine forest include red fir, lodgepole pine, western white pine, whitebark pine, and western juniper. Aspen sometimes occurs in small groves within this forest belt.

White fir is common at the lower elevations of this zone, but as you climb to higher, wetter sites, greater numbers of *red fir* are encountered. This species tends to be found on gentle slopes with moist soils. Snow depth under red fir stands averages ten to fifteen feet. Unlike other Sierran conifers, red fir often forms pure stands. Spot fires provide openings in the forest canopy that favor the development of red fir stands. Red fir's reddish, thick bark forms cathedral-like columns beneath dense, interlocking boughs. These shade the ground so that snow remains well into summer. The shade also results in nearly bare ground cover because few other plants can grow with so little light.

Lodgepole pine grows in the same areas as red fir but on shallower soils that are either too dry or too wet for the fir. It dominates glacially scoured basins and ridges and is often separated from other stands by great expanses of bare rock. In some places, lodgepole pine grows up to the altitudinal limit of trees. It also grows in boggy areas, such as the margins of lakes and meadows. It was this habit of growing in places that superficially resembled the habitat of eastern larch or tamarack that led some early Sierran residents to dub it "tamarack pine." Lodgepole pine is com-

Mountain hemlock, a species common in the Pacific Northwest, reaches its southern limits in the Yosemite region. This conifer can be identified by the drooping crown.

mon around the edges of Tuolumne Meadows and all along the Tioga Road east to Tioga Pass.

Lodgepole pine is the only pine in Yosemite with two-inch-long needles growing two to a bundle. It often grows in pure stands that reveal straight trunks covered by thin, papery, light brown bark. In the Rockies, this pine is often thin and spindly. It was used by the Plains tribes for tepee poles, hence its name. In the Sierra, lodgepole pine is frequently more robust. It can attain a girth of three feet or more and heights of a hundred feet. Because of the generally poor growing conditions found on the sites it tends to occupy, few plants are found beneath lodgepole pine. The most common understory plants are red mountain heath and Labrador tea.

Many lodgepole pines have serotinous cones; these are sealed by a waxy

In Yosemite, western white pine, which tends to grow in open stands near timberlines, is relatively easy to identify by its scaly bark, bundles of five needles, and rather long cones.

coating that prevents them from opening until heated. This is one reason why lodgepole pine dominates burned sites. The heat from a blaze helps to ensure prolific seed releases. Not all lodgepole cones on any particular tree are serotinous, however. Thus lodgepole can also regenerate in the absence of fire.

In the Rocky Mountains lodgepole pine appears to be dependent on fire for maintenance on a site; however, in the Sierra Nevada fire is less important. Here, lodgepole pine appears to be the climax species on many sites. This is due to the low productivity of most sites and consequent slow buildup of fuels, coupled with the extensive areas of bare rock that tend to isolate timber stands by acting as natural fire breaks. There have been no crown fires in Yosemite's lodgepole pine forests since record keeping begin in 1931.

Lodgepole pines have invaded many of the subalpine meadows in Yosemite. Studies indicate that much of this invasion began shortly after domestic livestock grazing was terminated. Apparently, the compaction of soil and disturbance of ground cover caused by thousands of hooves had allowed lodgepole seedlings to become established in subalpine areas.

Groves of *aspen*, the only deciduous species common outside of the riparian zone, are interspersed throughout the conifer zone nearly to timberline. Aspens tend to grow in wet meadows and in rock piles or other places where subsurface water is near the surface. Aspen is easily distinguished by its smooth, white bark. Its heart-shaped leaves flutter in the breeze, giving rise to one of its common names, "quaking aspen."

Aspen tends to form pure stands because it grows in genetically related clones. Its roots produce suckers after the mature trunk is killed. These suckers often number in the tens of thousands per acre. Although aspens produce hundreds of thousands of seeds each year, the seeds are so tiny that they almost never have enough stored food to put down a root and establish themselves before they run out of energy or die of dehydration. As a result, nearly all aspens in the West are thought to have regenerated from root suckers for thousands of years.

Mountain hemlock trees are relatively rare in Yosemite. This species is more common farther north, where cool, moist sites are more abundant. Growing near timberline in places where snow is abundant and deep, this graceful tree sports blue-green foliage on branches that extend nearly to the ground. A telltale way to distinguish it from other trees is by

Normally found on rocky, dry slopes and sometimes living a thousand years or more, western juniper trees often form gnarled, picturesque snags.

its drooping tip. Several groves of this tree are visible along the road between Tenaya Lake and Tuolumne Meadows. It is also visible near timberline on the trail to Mount Hoffman.

Another associate of the subalpine lodgepole pine/red fir forests is **western white pine**, which tends to grow on rocky ridges and well-drained sites. A five-needled pine with rusty red bark and upward-sweeping boughs, the western white pine has six- to ten-inch-long narrow cones that resemble the larger cones of sugar pine. In northern Idaho western white pine is a tall, graceful tree, but in the Sierra, it takes on a more squat form. One specimen measured by Porcupine Flat along the Tioga Road was eight feet across. A blister rust introduced from Europe has destroyed western white pine populations across the West; however, resistant strains are starting to repopulate areas where this species was once abundant.

At the limits to tree growth, around 10,000 feet, the most characteristic tree is **whitebark pine**. Although this tree is well known to hikers in the high country, within Yosemite it can only be seen from a road by Tioga Pass. With its airy, multibranched trunk, silver-gray bark, and two- to three-inch-round cones, this five-needled pine is relatively easy to identify.

Whitebark pine's large, edible seeds are gathered each summer and fall by the Clark's nutcracker. The bird removes the seeds from the cones and then caches them in the ground. During the winter and spring, it returns to dig out its stored food. Of course, it does not find all of the seeds, so some germinate to grow into new whitebark pines. Since the bird tends to hide the seeds on wind-swept ridges where snow depths are minimal, it's not surprising that many whitebark pines are found in such locations. When the trees die on these ridges, they produce beautiful, twisted, wind-sheared snags.

Whitebark pine's ability to persist at the limits to tree growth is enhanced by its tendency to assume a squat, stunted form. Each winter, shoots that stick up above the protective cover of snow are blasted by the wind; this kills the exposed branches. Eventually the tree takes on the appearance of a Japanese garden shrub. Under such stressful conditions, whitebark pine grows very slowly. John Muir once counted 426 growth rings in a whitebark pine whose trunk was only six inches in diameter.

Another, less common, member of the Sierra subalpine community is the **western juniper**. This gnarled, hardy tree extends its roots into cracks and crevices and appears to live on nothing more than rock. John Muir noted that western juniper seemed to live for centuries on "sunshine and snow." Despite the wind and common storms where it lives, some trees live a thousand years and develop a beautiful, weathered-polished appearance.

SUBALPINE MEADOWS

A distinctive feature of Yosemite's high country is the countless glades and openings. The best known and the largest subalpine, or montane, meadow in the entire Sierra Nevada is Tuolumne Meadows along the Tioga Road. Many of these meadows occur where the water table remains close to the surface throughout the growing season. Most trees cannot grow where their roots are continuously saturated. Meadows are common in glaciated basins where former lakes have filled in with sediments. Cold air drainage can also contribute to the persistence of meadows.

Unlike the grasses of the foothills, which are summer dormant, plants in subalpine meadows grow throughout the summer, perhaps because during the rest of the year they are under snow. Although most people assume these meadows are grasslands, the dominant plants are sedges. More than one hundred sedge species have been recorded for Sierran subalpine meadows. Sedges look like grasses but have leaves that are triangular in cross section instead of flat blades. The leaves of sedges also grow in ranks of three, instead of two as with grasses.

Despite the presence of sedges, a few grass species are also common. These include tufted hairgrass, short hairgrass, and spike trisetum.

Many of the mountain meadows of the Sierra Nevada suffered tremendous damage as a consequence of livestock grazing. It was the damage caused by domestic sheep that initially motivated John Muir to lobby for the establishment of Yosemite National Park. Although the consequences of this past degradation may not be apparent, subtle changes were set in motion by this period of grazing. Some, such as the entrenched stream channels, are still visible to the trained eye.

Common flowers of the subalpine zone include many of the same species found in the lower mixed-conifer zone, as well as California cone-flower, shooting star, mountain pride, camas lily, rein orchid, false hellebore, mountain bluebell, pink monkeyflower, arrowhead groundsel, marsh marigold, larkspur, fireweed, Davidson's fritillary, Sierra forget-me-not,

Lembert Dome, an example of a roche moutonnée, can be seen across Tuolumne Meadows. The dome is named for John Lembert, who settled in Tuolumne Meadows sometime before 1882. Overridden by a glacier, the dome has one gentle slope and one steep and rough.

The large leaves of false hellebore, a member of the lily family, are a common sight in wet meadows throughout the middle elevations of the park.

western columbine, paintbrush, wild iris, mules-ears, pearly everlasting, spreading phlox, wild geranium, scarlet gilia, meadow aster, mountain heather, whorled penstemon, arnica, mountain pennyroyal, wallflower, elephant head, Sierra gentian, purple monkshood, meadow rue, and little leopard lily. Shrubs of this zone include red osier dogwood, serviceberry, cream bush, labrador tea, spiraea, shrubby cinquefoil, pine mat manzanita, Sierra currant, dogbane, and bitter cherry.

Alpine Communities

Subalpine and alpine meadows are similar in many respects. Both experience short growing seasons, high insolation, and frigid temperatures most of the year. In Yosemite, vegetation occurring above 10,500 feet is considered alpine. Some plants grow up to the summits of the highest peaks. I've seen sky pilot growing on the 13,000-foot summit of Mount Dana.

Although superficially similar to the Arctic, the alpine regions of the Sierra have some distinctive features. Yosemite's alpine zone is sunnier and drier than the alpine areas of the Rockies and mountains farther north. The summer drought has favored adaptations to aridity. Many of the Sierran alpine plants are desert species that have moved upslope.

Alpine vegetation is sparse and short, interrupted by great expanses of rock. Alpine plants tend to be low to the ground; cushions or mats like spreading phlox and moss campion take advantage of the ground's warmth. Low stature also reduces damage from wind abrasion and reduces water losses to evaporation. Many alpine plants like alpine buckwheat have short hairs that further lessen water loss and keep the plant warm. The blossoms of alpine flowers are relatively large. For example, the blossom of alpine gold, a sunflower, is two inches across, though the entire plant is barely eight inches tall. This attracts insect pollinators and ensures adequate seed production.

Whereas many species of the foothills are annuals, most alpine plants are perennials, an adaptation to the limited growing season. Most plants simply do not have enough time to grow, flower, and produce seeds in the short alpine growing season. In fact, many plants in this zone take up to ten or more years to store sufficient energy to flower. Nevertheless, 6 percent of the Sierran alpine species are annuals; most of these are desert species that have migrated upslope where they invaded dry alpine areas. Many alpine plants can also reproduce vegetatively. This is insurance against bad seed crops or other adverse conditions.

Common alpine plants, such as this mountain heather, do not grow very tall. Their low stature allows them to benefit from the ground's warmth, protects them from wind, and lessens water loss.

Another adaptation that allows alpine plants to survive where the growing season is so short is their ability to photosynthesize at lower temperatures than their lowland counterparts. Finally, alpine vegetation can withstand freezing.

Species likely to be seen in the alpine zone include white heather, red mountain heather, shrubby cinquefoil, rock fringe, mountain sorrel, elephant head, alpine paintbrush, alpine gentian, swamp onion, American laurel, alpine penstemon, alpine daisy, alpine gold, grass of Parnassus, campion, western roseroot, alpine buckwheat, sky pilot, steer's head, spreading phlox, and alpine forget-me-not.

Alien Plants

A growing problem in Yosemite and throughout the West is biological pollution, or the loss of native species and genetic races to widely distributed alien plants. A recent survey found that eighty-four species, or 18 percent, of the plant species in Yosemite Valley are exotics. Some are quite common and naturalized, like Kentucky bluegrass, which dominates many of the meadows, while others, like the apple trees planted in the valley, will eventually disappear. Many were deliberately introduced during the era of livestock grazing for hay or grain production. This invasion of aliens is of concern because national parks are supposed to be managed for native species and preservation of native biodiversity. Alien plants usurp habitat that would otherwise support native species.

STATUS OF WILDLIFE

The biotic richness of Yosemite National Park stems from its pronounced elevation gradients and the resulting habitat diversity. From dry, arid, grassy foothills to alpine tundra on the highest peaks, Yosemite supports an estimated 247 birds, 80 mammals, and 1,400 species of flowering plants, shrubs, and trees.

Not all of Yosemite's native wildlife has survived into the present century. The last grizzly bear was killed in 1895, and the last bighorn disappeared from Yosemite's high country in 1914. Chinook salmon no longer run up the Merced River. Wolves are gone from Yosemite as well. Recently bighorns were reintroduced, and they appear to be doing well. And there is no good reason why wolves and grizzlies could not at some future date be reintroduced into the Sierra as well. Changes like these will require a new perspective about wildlife and ecosystem integrity, but Yosemite will never be whole nor complete until we restore all its ecological processes and components. This, at least, should be the goal. Often the most difficult part of such restoration is having the imagination to dare to dream of such a future. While the grizzly, salmon, and wolf await their turn, the process of ecological recovery in Yosemite continues—and the dream becomes more of a reality.

Changes in Status of Wildlife in Yosemite Valley

Many changes have occurred in the abundance and distribution of wildlife in Yosemite Valley as a result of human activities. Fire suppression has changed the vegetation. For example, black oak, a species favored by fire, has suffered a 90 percent decline in the valley since the park's establishment. Some species, like the great gray owl, are sensitive to human activities and no longer live in the valley. Others like the chinook salmon have disappeared as a consequence of habitat changes outside of the park. A few species, such as the brown-headed cowbird, have increased as a result of human influences. The following list documents changes in the distribution and abundance of selected Yosemite Valley species. Some of these species still breed in other parts of the park.

Species	Status	Last Documented Breeding or Occurrence
FISHES		
Chinook salmon	No longer occurs	?
Steelhead	No longer occurs	?
Brown trout	Introduced in 1897	
BIRDS		
Harlequin duck	No longer breeds	1925
Wood duck	No longer breeds	1943
Common merganser	No longer breeds	1939
Hooded merganser	Winter visitor	1940
Peregrine falcon	Declining overall, now experiencing slight recovery	Still occurs
Sharp-shinned hawk	No longer breeds	1930
Cooper's hawk	No longer breeds	1937
Virginia rail	No longer breeds	1943
Long-eared owl	No longer breeds	1915
Northern saw-whet owl	No longer breeds	1926
Great gray owl	No longer breeds	?
Belted kingfisher	Declining	Still occurs
Acorn woodpecker	Declining	Still occurs
Downy woodpecker	Declining	Still occurs
Willow flycatcher	No longer breeds	1966
Blue-gray gnatcatcher	No longer breeds	1924
Solitary vireo	Declining	Common in 1920s
Swainson's thrush	No longer breeds	Common in 1920s
Warbling vireo	Declining	Common in 1915
Yellow warbler	Declining	Common in 1915

Species	Status	Last Documented Breeding or Occurrence
Lazuli bunting	Reduced	Fairly common in 1930s
Chipping sparrow	Reduced	Common in 1920s
Lincoln's sparrow	No longer breeds	1923
Steller's jay	Increasing; common	
Brewer's blackbird	Increasing; common	
Brown-headed cowbird	Increasing; common	1934
Song sparrow	Increasing; common	
MAMMALS		
Spotted bat	Reduced	1959
Greater western mastiff bat	Reduced	1959
Fisher	No longer occurs	1920
River otter	No longer occurs	?
Wolf	No longer occurs	Likely occurred in past
Grizzly bear	No longer occurs	1895
Ringtail	Increasing; common	

FISHES

The waters of Yosemite support cold water fisheries. The most abundant and ubiquitous species are members of the trout family, thanks partly to human stocking efforts. Hatcheries were built at Wawona in 1895 and at Happy Isles in 1927 to provide fish for stocking Yosemite's waters, but historically, most lakes and streams above the 4,000-foot level were barren of fish.

Although the distribution of fish has expanded into high-elevation waters, other fish have disappeared from Yosemite. Chinook salmon and steelhead used to run up the Merced River into the park but disappeared as dams on the San Joaquin and tributaries wiped out the runs.

Six native fish species remain in the park. They include the Sacramento squawfish, hardhead, California roach, riffle sculpin, Sacramento sucker, and rainbow trout. Four other species, all trouts, have been introduced—brown trout, brook trout, cutthroat trout, and golden trout.

Trouts are the most widely distributed fishes in Yosemite. All trouts have similar diets, consisting of aquatic insects, small fish, frogs, and almost anything else that is small enough to eat and might fall into the water. Under favorable conditions all of the trout species in the park reach weights of ten pounds or more; however, the average fish is considerably smaller. Because of their willingness to strike artificial lures and their fighting qualities, trout are eagerly sought by anglers.

The policy of stocking lakes has largely been discontinued, but at least one hundred high-elevation lakes still have self-sustaining populations. Ironically, thirteen park lakes are still stocked, even though this is obviously inconsistent with the Park Service's policy of maintaining natural ecological process and species. Some biologists suspect that declines in park amphibians may be related to predation from introduced fish. (This is discussed in more detail in the amphibian section.)

The policy of allowing fishing should also be questioned, especially if sport fishing is used to justify stocking. Critics argue that we don't allow hunting in national parks, so why should fishing be encouraged? We don't kill deer or ground squirrels; should we kill fish? What impact does this have on fish-eaters like the otter or the mink? One can even question catch-and-release fishing. Would we permit people to lasso mule deer just for "fun," even if they were released apparently unharmed? Such questions of biology and ethics are bound to be explored in future years.

RAINBOW TROUT (Onchorhynchus mykiss, formerly Salmo gairdnerii)

Description. Back and tail blue to silver-gray fading to white on the belly. Back and upper portion of sides have black spots; a pale pink stripe along side gives rise to the name "rainbow."

Distribution. Only native trout species that originally occurred in Yosemite. Found in many lakes and rivers.

Remarks. Widely distributed throughout the world because of its fine qualities as a sport fish. Original distribution was limited to coastal rivers and waterways draining into the Pacific between Mexico and Alaska. Wild rainbows spawn in the spring. In the cold waters of Yosemite, a one-year-old fish may be only three to four inches long.

BROWN TROUT (Salmo trutta)

Description. Olive brown back fading to golden or yellow on sides. Belly white. Spotted like the rainbow; however, spots larger and darker, some with orange or red edges.

Distribution. Introduced into the United States from Europe. Planted in Sierran waters as early as 1895.

Remarks. Known as a crafty fish, more difficult to catch than other trout. Fall spawner.

CUTTHROAT TROUT (Onchorhynchus clarki, formerly Salmo clarki)

Description. Red slash under throat gives rise to name. Heavily dotted with black spots like rainbow.

Distribution. Native to the eastern side of the Sierra Nevada, but introduced west of the Sierran crest into Yosemite waters.

Remarks. Spring spawner. Sometimes hybridizes with rainbow trout where ranges overlap.

BROOK TROUT *(Salvelinus fontinalis)*

Description. Small scales, dark green back with dark wavy lines. Red spots on sides; some spots with blue borders. Pelvic and anal fins edged with white.

Distribution. Native to the eastern United States; transplanted into many western waters.

Remarks. Not a true trout; a member of the char family, which includes lake trout, arctic char, and Dolly Varden. Fall spawner. Ability to spawn in mountain lakes that lack tributaries is one reason for its success.

GOLDEN TROUT *(Onchorhynchus mykiss aguabonita,* formerly *Salmo aguabonita)*

Description. Similar to its close relative the rainbow trout. Pink lateral stripe present, but spots larger and less abundant. Pelvic and anal fins edged with white.

Distribution. Once restricted to the Kern River drainage in the southern Sierra. Has been transplanted to many other high mountain locations throughout the West.

Remarks. Spring spawner. Grows well in high-elevation lakes. Considered an endangered species in Kern River basin.

SACRAMENTO SUCKER *(Catostomus occidentalis)*

Description. Slender body with forked tail. Generally dark back and pale, creamy belly. Up to twenty-four inches long.

Distribution. Common in low-elevation streams like the Merced and Tuolumne rivers.

Remarks. Indians sought this fish by setting traps in rivers. Named for its sucker-shaped mouth and habit of vacuuming stream bottoms for food. Grazes rocks for algae. Lacks teeth.

SACRAMENTO SQUAWFISH *(Ptychocheilus grandis)*

Description. Long, streamlined body with forked tail. Large mouth extends to the eye. Silvery below and brownish green along back. Black spot near tail on young individuals.

Distribution. Found at lower elevations of major rivers.

Remarks. Member of the minnow family, but unlike most minnows reaches four feet in length. Eats insects, fish, and amphibians.

HARDHEAD (*Mylopharodon conocephalus*)

Description. Body long; head broad. Brownish green above and lighter below. Length up to three feet.

Distribution. Restricted to the lower elevations of rivers like the Merced.

Remarks. Member of minnow family. Feeds on insects and plant material.

CALIFORNIA ROACH (*Hesperoleucus symmetricus*)

Description. Very small mouth. Tail deeply forked; pectoral fins typically orange. Barely exceeds five inches in length.

Distribution. Common in low-elevation streams.

Remarks. Feeds mostly on insects and aquatic invertebrates.

RIFFLE SCULPIN (*Cottus gulosus*)

Description. Broad, rounded head tapers abruptly to narrow tail. Large pectoral fins an adaptation for maintaining position in swift mountain streams. Seldom more than two to three inches in length.

Distribution. Most swift streams at lower elevations in park, including Merced and Tuolumne rivers.

Remarks. Darts from rock to rock in swift, shallow streams.

AMPHIBIANS AND REPTILES

More than forty species of frogs, salamanders, turtles, lizards, and snakes are thought to occur in Yosemite. Except for the poisonous western rattlesnake, the park's amphibians and reptiles are harmless.

Both amphibians and reptiles are cold-blooded. They absorb warmth from the environment in order to remain active, and they hibernate, or become inactive, in colder weather.

Salamanders, frogs, and toads are amphibians. They have moist, glandular skins and lack external scales. Most adult amphibians are terrestrial, but amphibian eggs are normally laid in water. A few species of salamanders lay their eggs in damp areas, however.

Unlike amphibians, reptiles are completely adapted to life on land. There are three groups of reptiles—turtles, lizards, and snakes. They have dry, scaly skins and lay eggs. Like bird eggs, reptilian eggs have shells that prevent desiccation. Unlike amphibians, which can breathe through their moist skins, reptiles utilize only their lungs for respiration.

Amphibians

Salamanders
Salamanders have long, tailed bodies and moist skin. They prefer moist habitats and are seldom seen abroad except in spring when the woods are wet. Two species—the Mount Lyell salamander and the limestone salamander—are found almost no place else in the world except the Yosemite region.

CALIFORNIA NEWT *(Taricha torosa)*

Description. Reddish in color with vivid orange belly.

Distribution. Ranges up to 6,000 feet in the blue oak savanna and lower mixed coniferous forests, typically in riparian habitats. Requires ponds, lakes, or streams.

Remarks. Breeds between March and June. Eggs are attached to aquatic vegetation or placed in moist crevices under rocks. Inactive during the late summer and early fall; remains in burrows or crevices until rainy weather arrives.

MOUNT LYELL SALAMANDER *(Hydromantes platycephalus)*

Description. Spotted coloration matches the salt-and-pepper patterns of granite in its habitat.

Distribution. Rocky areas at the edges of snowbanks, wet meadows, and lakes.

Remarks. Named for Mount Lyell, the highest point in Yosemite Park. One of the few salamanders found above timberline. Restricted, or endemic, to the Sierra Nevada.

LIMESTONE SALAMANDER *(Hydromantes brunus)*

Description. Head and body flattened. Brown above; pale beneath. Five inches long.

Distribution. Very limited. Common only along riparian areas of the Merced River canyon where limestone outcrops occur. Seldom found above 2,500 feet.

Remarks. Not discovered until 1952. Very rare. Mushroom-like tongue can be extended up to one-third of its body length to capture prey.

ENSATINA *(Ensatina eschscholtzi)*

Description. Mottled black and orange with constriction at base of tail. Six inches long.

Distribution. Common throughout the middle elevations of the Sierra. Prefers areas under moist leaves and logs or inside rotted logs in mountain meadows or mixed coniferous forests.

Remarks. Does not require open water to lay eggs. Female sometimes protects eggs from dehydration by wrapping her body around them.

CALIFORNIA SLENDER SALAMANDER *(Batrachoseps attenuatus)*

Description. Yellowish or brownish stripe down back. Remainder of body dark gray. Eyes protrude.

Distribution. Found up to 5,000 feet in blue oak woodlands and chaparral.

Remarks. Often coils like a snake. When disturbed either flees rapidly or remains immobile as if dead.

RELICTUAL SLENDER SALAMANDER *(Batrachoseps relictus)*

Description. Slender, worm-like body. Generally gray with white freckles.

Distribution. Occurs from the Merced River canyon southward in the Sierra up to 8,000 feet. Inhabits moist mountain meadows, black oak/ponderosa pine woodlands, and riparian zones.

Remarks. Unlike other salamanders remains active during summer drought. Accomplishes this by remaining near moist crevices and seeps.

ARBOREAL SALAMANDER *(Aneides lugubris)*

Description. Wedge-shaped head distinctive. Typically brown above, sometimes with small yellow spots. Up to six inches long.

Distribution. Occasionally found in trees, particularly interior live oak, but usually found on the ground in black oak/ponderosa pine woodlands, riparian zones, and blue oak/pine savanna.

Remarks. Although most salamanders are silent, sometimes emits a squeak. Eats insects like other salamanders, but also consumes fungi.

Frogs and Toads

Although tadpoles are tailed, adult toads and frogs lack tails and have large hind legs designed for leaping and hopping. Frogs are distinguished from toads by their generally longer legs, smoother skins (which lack warts), and superior swimming ability. Toads tend to be stockier than frogs and to hop rather than leap. Their conspicuous warts secrete chemicals that are toxic to predators.

WESTERN TOAD (Bufo boreas)

Description. Brownish; distinguished by thin, whitish line running along center of back. Five inches long.

Distribution. Ranges from foothills up to subalpine forests at around 10,000 feet. Associated with mountain meadows and riparian areas.

Remarks. Produces a foul-tasting, milky fluid that discourages predators. Comes out at night to feed on insects, but hides in burrows during the hot, dry hours of the day.

YOSEMITE TOAD (Bufo canorus)

Description. Olive green; black blotches on females. About three inches long.

Distribution. Restricted to the central Sierra between 6,000 and 11,500 feet. Common in subalpine meadows fringed by lodgepole pine.

Remarks. Males have sustained melodious trill. Unlike most toads, sings in the daytime, an adaptation to its high-elevation habitat where low nighttime temperatures hinder activity.

PACIFIC TREEFROG (Hyla regilla)

Description. Distinguished by its small size (two inches long). Dark line runs from nose through eye.

Distribution. Widest elevational range of any amphibian in the Sierra; ranges from the Central Valley to 13,000 feet.

Remarks. Small, adhesive discs on toes are an adaptation to its tree-climbing habit. Unlike other frogs and toads, sings throughout the summer, not just during the mating season.

RED-LEGGED FROG (Rana aurora)

Description. Named for reddish legs and feet. Up to five inches.

Distribution. Blue oak savanna along riparian areas. Once found up to 6,000 feet, but seldom occurs that high any longer.

Remarks. Largest native frog in Sierra Nevada. Range has been greatly reduced as a result of competition from introduced bullfrog.

FOOTHILLS YELLOW-LEGGED FROG *(Rana boylei)*

Description. Color of back depends upon the background frog is resting upon. Lower belly and hind legs light yellow.
Distribution. Foothill riparian areas up to 6,000 feet.
Remarks. Disappearing from much of its range.

MOUNTAIN YELLOW-LEGGED FROG *(Rana muscosa)*

Description. Brown with blotches. Lower belly and inside of hind legs dark yellow. Three inches long.
Distribution. Common in higher elevations of the Sierra. Associated with mountain meadows, ponds, and riparian areas.
Remarks. Produces a musky smell when handled. Numbers have declined significantly; this is thought to be a consequence of predation by trout introduced into alpine lakes.

Reptiles

Turtles
Turtle bodies are encased in a protective shell into which the head and legs can be withdrawn when the turtle is alarmed. The jaws lack teeth.

WESTERN POND TURTLE *(Clemmys marmorata)*

Description. Greenish brown shell; yellow belly with dark spots.
Distribution. Up to 6,000 feet but primarily in foothills.
Remarks. Seldom leaves water. Can remain submerged for several minutes. Survives long periods of drought by burrowing, but usually associated with permanent water. Eats aquatic plants and insects. The only turtle found in the western Sierra.

Lizards
Lizards are shaped like salamanders but live in dry habitats. Like snakes they use their tongues to smell, flicking them to pick up prey's scent.

WESTERN FENCE LIZARD *(Sceloporus occidentalis)*

Description. Blue belly and throat; brownish gray blotches on back.

Distribution. From blue oak savanna up through mixed conifer forests to 9,000 feet.

Remarks. Blue throat and belly used to establish territories and attract mates. Feeds primarily on insects.

SAGEBRUSH LIZARD *(Sceloporus graciosus)*

Description. Back brown with large, dark blotches; throat and belly may be light blue.

Distribution. Despite its name, common in forested habitats between 6,000 and 9,000 feet.

Remarks. Does rapid push-ups when agitated.

GILBERT'S SKINK *(Eumeces gilberti)*

Description. Head orange; trunk greenish brown. Young skink has blue tail. Eight inches long.

Distribution. Primarily foothills up to 6,500 feet in black oak woodlands and chaparral.

Remarks. Can grow a new tail to replace one lost to predator.

WESTERN WHIPTAIL LIZARD *(Cnemidophorus tigris)*

Description. Pointed snout; tiger-like markings on back and sides.

Distribution. Hot, dry grasslands, chaparral, and stand of digger pine or oak up to 7,500 feet.

Remarks. Very fast. Moves with jerky motion.

SOUTHERN ALLIGATOR LIZARD *(Gerrhonotus multicarinatus)*

Description. Green to reddish body. Dark stripes on belly run along middle of scale rows. Up to twelve inches in length.

Distribution. Mostly foothills including chaparral and mixed coniferous forests up to 6,000 feet.

Remarks. When surprised sometimes runs at attacker with mouth wide open to bluff predator. Tail breaks off if grabbed by predator.

NORTHERN ALLIGATOR LIZARD (Gerrhonotus coeruleus)

Description. Dark with blotched greenish gray skin. Dark stripes on belly aligned between scale rows.

Distribution. Unlike most lizards, which are restricted to lower elevations, prefers forested areas up to 11,000 feet.

Remarks. Eggs retained inside the female; young born alive. This is an adaptation to cold, high-elevation habitats. Occasionally takes to water to escape a predator.

Snakes

Snakes are legless reptiles that lack eyelids. They move by alternately contracting groups of muscles to produce a side-to-side motion. Snakes are adapted to preying upon small mammals, insects, frogs, and other animals. Their unhinged jaws allow them to swallow large prey with ease.

RUBBER BOA (Charina bottae)

Description. Brown with smooth skin and small, blunt head. Up to thirty inches long.

Distribution. Meadows in forested areas from 5,000 to 9,000 feet.

Remarks. Fused bones in head aid in burrowing. Like other boas, usually kills its prey (birds and rodents) by constriction.

RINGNECK SNAKE (Diadophis punctatus)

Description. Red-orange neck band encircles black head. Back bluish green; belly reddish. Up to eighteen inches in length.

Distribution. Damp places in foothills, often on north-facing slopes up to 6,000 feet.

Remarks. Eats salamanders, frogs, and lizards.

SHARP-TAILED SNAKE (Contia tenuis)

Description. Named for sharp spine at end of tail. Reddish brown. Up to fourteen inches long.

Distribution. Riparian deciduous areas and meadows up to 7,000 feet.
Remarks. Eats salamanders, snails, and slugs.

RACER (Coluber constrictor)

Description. Blue-gray body. Belly yellow; eyes large. Fifty inches long.
Distribution. From grasslands and blue oak savanna up to forests at 6,000 feet.
Remarks. Considered the fastest snake. Can keep up with a running person. Aggressive; bites if cornered.

STRIPED RACER (Masticophis lateralis)

Description. Black to dark brown with creamy yellow stripe along each side of back. Up to sixty inches in length.
Distribution. Foothills along streams.
Remarks. Enters trees and shrubs to obtain bird eggs and nestlings.

GOPHER SNAKE (Pituophis melanoleucus)

Description. Brown with dark blotches on back. Resembles rattlesnake. Up to seven feet in length.
Distribution. Up to 7,000 feet in blue oak savanna, chaparral, and mixed coniferous forests.
Remarks. Rattles tail in dry leaves to imitate the buzz of a rattler. Squeezes prey and swallows it whole.

COMMON KINGSNAKE (Lampropeltis getulus)

Description. Alternating black and white bands. Up to sixty inches long.
Distribution. Forested habitat up to 6,000 feet.
Remarks. Attacks and eats rattlesnakes. Immune to rattlesnake poison. Also eats small mammals, frogs, lizards, and birds.

MOUNTAIN KINGSNAKE (Lampropeltis zonata)

Description. Brightly colored with red, white, and black bands. Up to forty inches long.

Distribution. Up to 8,000 feet in moist, cool canyons in forested areas.
Remarks. Eats small lizards, snakes, and birds.

COMMON GARTER SNAKE (*Thamnophis sirtalis*)

Description. Dark back; prominent yellow stripe with small red blotches along sides. Up to fifty inches long.
Distribution. Common along streams up to 6,000 feet.
Remarks. Forages for fish, frogs, and small rodents. Inflates body and emits foul-smelling fluid when alarmed.

WESTERN TERRESTRIAL GARTER SNAKE (*Thamnophis elegans*)

Description. Dark back with whitish side stripes. Up to forty-two inches long.
Distribution. Streams and lakes at higher elevations than the common garter snake.
Remarks. Feeds on tadpoles, frogs, and fish. Most common reptile in high Sierra. Female retains eggs inside body to provide additional warmth—an adaptation to its cold, high-elevation habitat. Young born alive.

WESTERN AQUATIC GARTER SNAKE (*Thamnophis couchi*)

Description. Dark brown body, light belly; sides not red. Up to fifty inches long.
Distribution. Rivers and streams throughout foothills.
Remarks. Excellent swimmer. Eats tadpoles, frogs, and fish. Young born alive in late summer.

NIGHT SNAKE (*Hypsiglena torquata*)

Description. Light brown with dark brown blotches. Large brown spots on sides of neck. Vertical pupils. Up to twenty inches long.
Distribution. Foothills, particularly in chaparral.
Remarks. Nocturnal as name implies. Venomous but not harmful to humans.

WESTERN RATTLESNAKE (*Crotalus viridis*)

Description. Stout body with rattle on tail. Brown with blotches. Head broad and flat.

Distribution. Up to 11,000 feet. Typically found in rock piles.

Remarks. Eats rodents, primarily ground squirrels. Like some of the garter snakes, female western rattler retains fertilized eggs in body, and young are born alive. At one time rattlesnakes were killed in Yosemite, but like all wildlife in the park they are now protected, something that John Muir advocated more than a hundred years ago.

BIRDS

Active in daylight hours, birds are the most obvious and easily observed wildlife in the park. Bird watching is Yosemite's number one outdoor activity, surpassing fishing, hunting, and other outdoor endeavors.

Evolution and Adaptations

Birds evolved from reptiles. You can see this resemblance in the scaly skin they still retain on their legs. The feathers of birds evolved from modified scales. Feathers were a significant step forward. Not only did they make flight possible; the insulation provided by feathers also allowed birds to become warm-blooded.

Flight required more than just the development of feathers. Birds had to become less dense than their reptilian ancestors. Other evolutionary changes included a beak that replaced heavy teeth; lightweight, hollow bones; and wings, which developed from the forelimbs.

Because of the energy demands of flight, most birds require high-energy diets. Concentrated energy sources like insects, nectar, and seeds dominate bird diets.

Songs

Birds communicate in many ways; however, song is usually the most obvious means. Bird songs are complex arrangements of many individual sounds—up to eighty notes per second—that sound like single notes to our untrained ears. Songs are most often heard during the breeding season, when males attempt to attract mates and to advertise territorial boundaries.

Birds communicate with other birds in a flock. Chickadees and some other birds that move in small flocks call frequently as they forage in dense vegetation. These location calls help keep the flock together.

Low sounds carry farther in dense vegetation than high ones. This is one reason why the call of the blue grouse, an inhabitant of dense forests, has a low, booming hoot. The same is true for owls like the great horned owl that typically live in forested areas.

Diet

A bird's behavior, body shape, and habitat determine its food preferences. Research has shown that birds move into an area and monitor things like insect abundance to determine whether to nest there or not. Since insect abundance varies with weather and other factors from year to year, bird distribution and abundance change annually as well.

Seeds are nutritious, abundant, and slightly less prone to year-to-year variation than insects. Therefore, many Sierran birds eat seeds during at least part of the year. Birds like the Clark's nutcracker, rosy finch, and red crossbill, which specialize on seeds, tend to have stout bills to help them crack hard seed coats. Young of seed eaters are typically fed insects, however, because insects are easier to eat and digest than seeds.

Some insect eaters, such as swifts, swallows, and flycatchers, are agile flyers and catch insects on the wing. Others, like warblers, forage for insects on the branches of shrubs and trees. Nuthatches and brown creepers search for insects on the trunks of trees.

Woodpeckers are among the most specialized insectivores. They drill through the bark of trees and pluck insect larvae and beetles from the wood. To survive their head-pounding activities, woodpeckers have reinforced skulls. Pointed, stout bills allow them to penetrate wood, and stiff tail feathers prop woodpeckers up on tree trunks. Their long and sticky tongues enable them to grip prey easily.

The smaller the bird, the larger its surface relative to the volume of its body and, consequently, the greater the heat loss. That is why small birds have higher energy demands and higher metabolic rates. A hummingbird's small body loses so much heat, for example, that it must eat nectar, a diet of almost pure sugar. And it even goes into torpor, cooling its own body at night, to reduce energy losses when it is not feeding.

Few birds are strict vegetarians, although some, like geese, consume mostly grass. This lack of herbivory is a result of the high energy demands placed on most birds and the low energy content of foods like grass. Most birds simply cannot survive on such a diet. The ones that do tend to be larger birds whose bulk enables them to minimize heat losses, thus reducing their overall energy requirements.

Cavity Nesters

Many kinds of birds are cavity nesters. These include woodpeckers like the northern flicker, hairy woodpecker, black-backed woodpecker, and pileated woodpecker as well as the mountain chickadee, common golden-eye, wood duck, white-breasted nuthatch, mountain bluebird, northern pygmy owl, and American kestrel.

Cavities are not abundant in the environment; thus, competition for suitable nest sites is great. The advantages to cavity nesters are significant, however. The young of cavity nesters are less exposed to the elements and to predators.

Cavities tend to be created in older, mature trees, often after the trees die. In areas with significant amounts of logging, cavities are particularly scarce. This underscores the importance of snag-creating agents like wildfire, pine beetles, and drought. Without dead trees, you don't get snags. To protect mountain bluebirds, you need to protect pine beetles. To ensure plenty of black-backed woodpeckers, you need to allow wildfires. You cannot support one without the other; fortunately in places like Yosemite such ecological processes are permitted to play out their special roles in the ecosystem.

Habitat Preferences of Park Birds

The National Park Service bird checklist for Yosemite lists 247 species that have been recorded within the boundaries of the park; however, some of these species are encountered only infrequently.

Some species merely pass through Yosemite en route to breeding grounds elsewhere; others breed in the park but winter at lower elevations outside the park or migrate south to the tropics. Very few species are year-round residents. Included in the latter group are the mountain chickadee, chestnut-sided chickadee, golden-crowned kinglet, red-breasted nuthatch, white-breasted nuthatch, brown creeper, canyon wren, winter wren, American dipper, ruby-crowned kinglet, Townsend's solitaire, rufous-sided towhee, brown towhee, dark-eyed junco, rosy finch, common raven, Steller's jay, acorn woodpecker, northern goshawk, belted king-fisher, Williamson's sapsucker, Nuttall's woodpecker, downy woodpecker, white-headed woodpecker, northern flicker, black-backed woodpecker, pileated woodpecker, great horned owl, northern pygmy owl, northern saw-whet owl, spotted owl, and great gray owl.

Birds are mobile. Although some species are strongly associated with one habitat type, many others are habitat generalists or shift their use patterns throughout the year. This makes it difficult to generalize about bird habitat use. With this cautionary note in mind, we will examine some general patterns.

Foothills and Chaparral Zone

Snow is rare in the foothills, and spring and summer come early. By midsummer, the foothills are intensely hot and dry. Many birds nest here but abandon the zone later in the season. Oaks like the blue oak and chaparral species such as manzanita dominate this zone. In the spring, one may encounter ash-throated flycatchers, white-breasted nuthatches, scrub jays, rufous-sided towhees, blue-gray gnatcatchers, and acorn woodpeckers.

Transition Conifer Zone

The transition forest is the land of the black oak and ponderosa pine. This is the vegetation that dominates Yosemite Valley itself. Along the edge of the valley's meadows and pine forests live yellow-rumped warblers, olive-sided flycatchers, western wood pewees, white-crowned sparrows, dark-eyed juncos, chipping sparrows, and yellow warblers. Within the forests one may encounter hairy woodpeckers, brown creepers, red-breasted nuthatches, black-headed grosbeaks, Nashville warblers, and solitary vireos. Near campgrounds Steller's jay and Brewer's blackbird are ubiquitous.

Mixed Conifer Zone

Between 6,000 and 8,000 feet, one enters the mid-elevation forests dominated by conifers such as Jeffrey pine, sugar pine, white fir, red fir, and sequoia. In these forests, one finds western tanagers, hermit warblers, warbling vireos, pileated woodpeckers, and golden-crowned kinglets.

Subalpine Forest

The subalpine red fir forest forms shady groves that hold snow late into the summer. White fir, usually a species of mid-elevation forests, is sometimes also present in this forest. Lodgepole pine occurs at the upper limits of red fir forests. Here you are apt to see mountain chickadees, yellow-rumped warblers, and golden-crowned kinglets, or to hear the booming call of the blue grouse.

At the upper limits of the whitebark pine, mountain hemlock, and lodgepole forests live Clark's nutcrackers and dusky flycatchers. Rufous hummingbirds can be seen in subalpine meadows during the summer.

Alpine Zone

Snow covers the treeless alpine zone much of the year; however, during the brief summer growing season, a few hardy birds come to nest or forage. They include the water pipit, white-crowned sparrow, rosy finch, and an occasional mountain bluebird.

Species Accounts

The following species accounts provide a brief overview of some of the birds that are known to inhabit Yosemite National Park. Some are quite common; others are unusual. These accounts do not cover all the birds one may encounter in Yosemite. A more complete listing of all species is found in the Bird List. For more information, the visitor is encouraged to purchase a good birding guide. Serious birders might opt to obtain one or both of two excellent local bird books—*Birds of Yosemite and the East Slope*, by David Gaines, and *Discovering Sierra Birds*, by Edward Beedy and Stephen Granholm.

Ducks and Geese

Despite the abundance of alpine lakes and streams within the park, there is not much good habitat for ducks and geese. Nevertheless, several species are occasionally seen in Yosemite.

MALLARD *(Anas platyrhynchos)*

Description. Male: green head, white collar, chestnut breast, white belly. Female: drab brown.

Distribution. Along slow stretches of the Merced and Tuolumne rivers, Little Yosemite Valley, and Yosemite Valley.

Remarks. One of the most common ducks in North America. Like most ducks, mallard males seek new mates each year; showy plumage used to attract females. Mallards and other puddle ducks are able to jump directly into the air from resting position on water; puddle ducks can also walk well on land.

WOOD DUCK (Aix sponsa)

Description. Male: colorful plumage and head crest. Female: drab brown with white belly and teardrop-shaped eye patch.

Distribution. Along rivers, particularly where there are oaks. Formerly bred in Yosemite Valley.

Remarks. Cavity nester. Feeds on acorns; even flies into oak trees to forage. Also eats aquatic plants. Once more common, but loss of riparian habitat as a result of dams, livestock grazing, and other changes has greatly reduced numbers.

HARLEQUIN DUCK (Histrionicus histrionicus)

Description. Male: strikingly colorful—slate blue head and chest, bright orange-brown sides, white facial and body markings. Female: gray-brown with three white head spots.

Distribution. Turbulent Sierran streams. Historically bred along Tuolumne and Merced rivers. The only recent sightings have been in Tenaya Canyon and along South Fork of the Merced.

Remarks. Takes its name from brightly dressed clowns of medieval Europe. Once bred throughout the western slope but may now be extinct as a breeding population in the Sierra. Only three breeding records since 1927. If you see one, report it to park personnel.

BARROW'S GOLDENEYE (Bucephala islandica)

Description. Small with white wing patch. Male: greenish black head that appears shiny purple. White crescent in front of eye; belly and chest also white. Wings whistle when flock takes off.

Distribution. Formerly bred in Sierra from Yosemite Park northward.

Remarks. Cavity nester. Never common in Yosemite. No recent breeding records from the Sierra.

COMMON MERGANSER (Mergus merganser)

Description. Sleek profile and long, narrow, serrated bill. White flashing wing pattern shows in flight. Females have red head, males green.

Distribution. Nests in cavities along streams and lakes. Has nested in Yosemite Valley and Hetch Hetchy Canyon. Occasionally seen along rivers.

Remarks. Fish-eater; needs clear water in which to feed. Clumsy on land; requires a running start to get airborne.

Hawks and Eagles

Three groups of hawks occur in Yosemite. Accipiters, or forest hawks, include the northern goshawk, Cooper's hawk, and sharp-shinned hawk. Their rounded wings and pointed tails allow them to maneuver among trees. Buteos, or soaring hawks, such as the red-tailed hawk, have broad wings and short tails. They are birds of open country. Finally, falcons are built for speed; they have pointed wings and tails. Eagles are most like buteos in shape and habits. Ten species of hawks and eagles have been recorded in Yosemite, but only six are common enough to warrant descriptions. The peregrine falcon is also included because it is an endangered species.

NORTHERN GOSHAWK (*Accipiter gentilis*)

Description. Conspicuous white eyebrow; chest and belly white with gray barring; back slate gray; white fluffy feathers under tail.

Distribution. Mature to old-growth coniferous forests of middle elevations; Yosemite Valley, Tuolumne Meadows, Crane Flat, Wawona.

Remarks. Defends nest sites vigorously; attacks intruders. Hunts rodents and other birds, typically in forest settings.

COOPER'S HAWK (*Accipiter cooperii*)

Description. About the size of a crow. Long tail and short, rounded wings. Gray back and reddish barring on breast and belly; barring on tail.

Distribution. Breeds from blue oak/pine savanna up through black oak/ponderosa pine zone. Prefers oaks and riparian sites. Merced and Tuolumne river canyons and Crane Flat.

Remarks. Aggressively defends nest site. Small birds and rodents primary prey. Very maneuverable; captures other birds on the wing.

SHARP-SHINNED HAWK *(Accipiter striatus)*

Description. Smallest of accipiters; easily confused with Cooper's hawk. Sharpshin has smaller head and shorter neck.

Distribution. Riparian habitats of black oak/ponderosa pine zone up to red fir forests. Prefers mature trees. Yosemite Valley, Hetch Hetchy Canyon, Crane Flat.

Remarks. Small birds caught on the wing make up 97 percent of diet. Occasionally takes small rodents.

RED-TAILED HAWK *(Buteo jamaicensus)*

Description. Broad wings. Adult: reddish tail; belly light; dark brown barring across chest.

Distribution. Blue oak savanna up to alpine. Hunts in semiopen to open terrain. Common in appropriate habitats in Yosemite.

Remarks. Often soars. Feeds primarily on rodents.

GOLDEN EAGLE *(Aquila chrysaetos)*

Description. Adult: large brown body; broad tail. Seven-foot wingspread. Immature: white band on tail and white patches under wings.

Distribution. Open country from lowlands to alpine areas.

Remarks. Often soars scanning ground for prey. Builds bulky stick nests on cliffs. Nests reused from year to year, so they grow successively larger. Feeds on rabbits, pikas, marmots, and ground squirrels.

AMERICAN KESTREL *(Falco sparverius)*

Description. Pointed wings and long tail. Robin-sized. Males: bright reddish backs, slate blue wings. Females: rusty underparts.

Distribution. Open grasslands and meadows. Throughout park in suitable habitat up to Tuolumne Meadows.

Remarks. Cavity nester. Often hovers. Hunts grasshoppers, small birds, and rodents.

PEREGRINE FALCON *(Falco peregrinus)*

Description. Pointed wings and long tail. Adult: Slate gray above, whitish throat. Black mask over face, cheek, and eye.

Distribution. Very rare. Three nest sites recorded in Yosemite.

Remarks. Making a slow comeback after being devastated by DDT poisoning in the 1950s and 1960s. Feeds mostly on small birds captured on the wing.

Owls

These birds are the nighttime equivalent of hawks. They hunt small mammals, birds, and even insects. Their exceptional hearing permits them to capture prey in total darkness. Fluffy plumage on their wings makes owl flight nearly soundless. Eight species of owls are known for Yosemite, but the western screech owl and long-eared owl are so seldom seen they are not described below.

FLAMMULATED OWL *(Otus flammeolus)*

Description. The only small owl with dark eyes. Variegated reddish gray plumage. Less than seven inches long.

Distribution. Favors stands of ponderosa and Jeffrey pines in mid-elevation forests.

Remarks. Cavity nester. Eats moths and other insects.

GREAT HORNED OWL *(Bubo virginianus)*

Description. Large gray-brown owl with ear tufts and white throat.

Distribution. Foothills to subalpine areas. Recorded in Yosemite Valley, Tuolumne Meadows, Wawona, and Crane Flat.

Remarks. One of the earliest nesters; lays eggs in January. Small mammals make up 90 percent of diet.

NORTHERN PYGMY OWL *(Glaucidium gnoma)*

Description. Smallest Sierran owl. Long tail; small head that lacks ear tufts. Belly white with dark streaks; back brown to gray.

Distribution. Open woodlands mostly at lower elevations; seldom found above 6,000 feet.

Remarks. Cavity nester. Hunts in daytime as well as night.

SPOTTED OWL (Strix occidentalis)

Description. White spots on head and body; dark eyes.

Distribution. Dense coniferous old-growth forests from ponderosa pine zone to subalpine red fir forests. Recorded for Yosemite Valley, Wawona, and Crane Flat.

Remarks. Requires cool, shady habitat. Feeds on flying squirrels and wood rats.

GREAT GRAY OWL (Strix nebulosa)

Description. Large. Gray plumage; prominent facial discs. Lacks ear tufts.

Distribution. Rare in Sierra, although more abundant in Yosemite than elsewhere. Requires open meadows adjacent to forest.

Remarks. It is estimated that only thirty to forty great gray owls remain in all of California; nine have been found in Yosemite. Requires voles. Has declined because of livestock grazing outside park, which has devastated meadow habitat of its prey.

NORTHERN SAW-WHET OWL (Aegolius acadicus)

Description. Reddish streaks on breast; spots on back. Eight inches long.

Distribution. Dense forests from mixed conifers in the ponderosa pine belt up to edge of red fir. Recorded in Yosemite Valley, Merced Grove, and Crane Flat.

Remarks. Cavity nester. Silent most of the year; may be more abundant than casual observation would suggest. Relatively tame.

Chickenlike Birds

Grouse and other chickenlike birds have precocious young that are able to walk and feed themselves immediately after they hatch.

BLUE GROUSE (Dendragapus obscurus)

Description. Male: gray plumage; orangish eye stripe; dark tail with gray band. Female: mottled brown with dark tail. About twenty inches long.

Distribution. Mixed conifers to red fir forests. In Yosemite recorded from Mount Hoffman, Glacier Point, and Porcupine Flat.

Remarks. In spring, male has a ventriloquistic booming hoot. Young eat insects; adults survive on pine needles, buds, and cones.

WHITE-TAILED PTARMIGAN *(Lagopus leucurus)*

Description. Plumage brown in summer, pure white in winter. Tail remains white year-round.

Distribution. Among boulders in alpine tundra. Dana Plateau, Gaylor Lake, Matterhorn Peak.

Remarks. Associated with willows, its prime food source. Not native to California. Introduced at Mono Pass by California Department of Fish and Game in 1971. Has since spread north and south. One found near Mount Williamson, one hundred miles south of Yosemite.

MOUNTAIN QUAIL *(Oreortyx pictus)*

Description. Gray and brown above with two long head plumes. Reddish sides edged in white bars. Approximately eleven inches long.

Distribution. Chaparral mixed with grassy openings. Mariposa Grove, Yosemite Valley, Chinquapin.

Remarks. Makes spring-fall migrations of up to twenty miles—all on foot.

Sandpipers and Gulls

SPOTTED SANDPIPER *(Actitus macularia)*

Description. Breeding adult: brown back; white-spotted breast and belly; black eye stripe.

Distribution. Sandy or pebbly shorelines from foothills to subalpine zone. Tuolumne Meadows, Yosemite Valley.

Remarks. Teeters when walking.

CALIFORNIA GULL *(Larus californicus)*

Description. Adult: white head, gray back, white belly, black wing tips; yellow bill with red spot on tip.

Distribution. Tenaya Lake, Roosevelt Lake, Tioga Lake (just outside park).

Remarks. Second largest California gull colony in the world located at Mono Lake east of Yosemite. Water diversions threaten these birds.

Doves and Pigeons

Doves and pigeons are members of the same family. All are fast-flying birds.

BAND-TAILED PIGEON *(Columbia fasciata)*

Description. Purple head; dark-tipped yellow bill; gray tail and back.

Distribution. Oak woodlands and coniferous forests. Yosemite Valley, Big Oak Flat Road, Crane Flat, Mariposa Grove.

Remarks. Feeds on acorns. Travels in flocks.

MOURNING DOVE *(Zenaida macroura)*

Description. Long, tapering tail. White outer tips of tail feathers visible in flight.

Distribution. Chaparral; lower elevations of park. El Portal area.

Remarks. Rapid, strong flyer. Cooing males audible in spring and summer.

Swifts

These birds spend most of their days pursuing insects on the wing. Their long, pointed wings are built for speed. Three species, black, Vaux's, and white-throated swifts, have been recorded for Yosemite, but only the latter is abundant.

WHITE-THROATED SWIFT *(Aeronautes saxatalis)*

Description. Slightly forked tail, black back, white and black belly.

Distribution. Near rocky cliffs above water. Yosemite Falls, Vernal Falls, Bridalveil Fall, Merced and Tuolumne canyons.

Remarks. Exceptionally fast flyers.

Hummingbirds

These are the smallest birds in North America. Because their surface area is large in proportion to their small volume, hummingbirds lose heat to the environment rapidly. They counter this loss in two ways—by eating a high energy diet, and by going into torpor at night to reduce heat loss. Members of this group are important pollinators. Some flowers like penstemons and paintbrushes are designed to attract hummingbirds. Flowers pollinated by hummingbirds tend to be red. Four species of hummingbirds have been recorded for Yosemite, but only two are common.

CALLIOPE HUMMINGBIRD (Stellula calliope)

Description. Short tail and bill. Male: green above, white below; purple-red throat feathers. Female: green back, pinkish white belly. Smallest North American bird.

Distribution. Nests from ponderosa pine to red fir forests.

Remarks. Nest often strategically located under foliage to reduce nighttime radiation to cool sky.

RUFOUS HUMMINGBIRD (Selasphorus rufus)

Description. Male: reddish brown back. Female: green back, white belly.

Distribution. Throughout park up to alpine zone, but most common in ponderosa pine belt. Follows flowers upslope as they bloom.

Remarks. Does not nest in Yosemite. Passes through foothills during spring migration, breeds farther north, then passes back through Sierra Nevada in mid- to late summer on southward migration.

Kingfishers

Short, stocky birds with large heads and bills. Capture fish. Only one species in Yosemite.

BELTED KINGFISHER (Ceryle alcyon)

Description. Ragged crest; loud, rattling voice. Male: slate blue with white belly. Female: rusty belly stripe.

Distribution. Waterways including larger lakes, Tuolumne and Merced rivers.

Remarks. Perches or hovers above water, then dives for small fish, insects, frogs, and other prey.

Woodpeckers

Twelve species of woodpeckers are recorded for Yosemite, but Lewis' and Nuttall's woodpeckers are seldom seen in the park. Woodpeckers excavate nest cavities and search for insects in trees. Some species also drum on trees to mark territories.

ACORN WOODPECKER (*Melanerpes formicivorus*)

Description. Black chin, yellow throat, red cap, white cheeks and neck, black back, and white-spotted belly give clownlike appearance.

Distribution. Lives among oaks. Most common woodpecker in park.

Remarks. Like wolves adults form cooperative breeding groups. All group members help defend territory, but only one adult pair breeds. Birds cache extra acorns in large oaks or posts. Granaries may hold ten thousand acorns.

RED-BREASTED SAPSUCKER (*Sphyrapicus ruber*)

Description. Red head, nape, and breast; white wing bar, yellowish belly, black back. Eight and one-half inches long.

Distribution. Common in mixed conifers near stream or meadows.

Remarks. Drills horizontal rows of holes in living trees to get sap.

WILLIAMSON'S SAPSUCKER (*Sphyrapicus thyroideus*)

Description. Male: black back, white rump, white wing patch. Female: brown back, white rump, no white wing patch.

Distribution. Subalpine forests, particularly lodgepole pine.

Remarks. Drills holes in irregular pattern. Feeds on cambium layer and sap. Feeds ants to young.

DOWNY WOODPECKER (*Picoides pubescens*)

Description. White back; black cheek patch, wings, and nape; red crown; white belly. Small bill. Six and three-quarters inches long.

Distribution. Streamside willows, alders, and maples. Yosemite Valley, Foresta.

Remarks. Smallest woodpecker in North America.

HAIRY WOODPECKER *(Picoides villosus)*

Description. Similar to downy woodpecker, but stouter bill, half as long as head. Up to nine inches long.

Distribution. Prefers old-growth forests or recent burns in mixed coniferous forests. Resident in winter.

Remarks. Eats bark beetles and other insects. Occasionally eats pine seeds in winter.

WHITE-HEADED WOODPECKER *(Picoides albolarvatus)*

Description. Head white; back black. Male: red patch on back of head.

Distribution. Strongly associated with mixed coniferous forests, especially stands of ponderosa pine and sugar pine.

Remarks. Pine seeds make up 60 percent of diet; insects, 40 percent.

NORTHERN FLICKER *(Colaptes auratus)*

Description. Spotted breast, red wing linings, brown barred back. Male: red mustache. About twelve and one-half inches long.

Distribution. Open forests with patches of meadows or bare ground. Found throughout the park.

Remarks. Obtains most food on the ground; avoids deep snow. Eats mainly ants and other ground insects.

PILEATED WOODPECKER *(Dryocopus pileatus)*

Description. Red crest, black body, white stripe on face and shoulder. White wing linings. Loud drumming heard great distances. Nearly seventeen inches in length.

Distribution. Old-growth forests of mixed forest zone up to red fir. Yosemite Valley, Mariposa Grove, Crane Flat, Wawona.

Remarks. Requires large dead snags to survive. Populations have declined outside of park because of logging. Important cavity excavator; its large holes are used by wood ducks, mergansers, flying squirrels, and other animals.

Flycatchers

These small, drab birds capture insects in midair. Flycatchers perch on branches and dart out to scoop up their prey. Typically they have whiskers about the face; these are thought to protect the eyes from insects that are missed during a swoop. Ten species of flycatchers are recorded for Yosemite, but only four are relatively common.

OLIVE-SIDED FLYCATCHER *(Nuttallornis borealis)*

Description. Small and grayish with white tufts on each side of rump.

Distribution. Common in mid-elevation forests. Prefers scattered, mature forests up to subalpine zone.

Remarks. Perches in tallest trees, from which it makes swooping forays to capture flying insects.

WESTERN WOOD PEWEE *(Contopus sordidulus)*

Description. Small, grayish olive bird with dull white throat.

Distribution. One of the most widespread birds in Sierra. Nests in nearly every habitat up to subalpine zone.

Remarks. Perches in trees; captures insects in nearby meadows or other openings.

HAMMOND'S FLYCATCHER *(Empidonax hammondii)*

Description. Almost impossible to distinguish from dusky flycatcher. White eye ring; gray head and back; grayish white throat; yellowish belly.

Distribution. Shady forests from mixed conifers to red fir zone.

Remarks. Common summer resident.

DUSKY FLYCATCHER *(Empidonax oberholseri)*

Description. Gray above, yellowish below; white throat.

Distribution. Prefers open mixed coniferous forests with shrubby understory.

Remarks. Sometimes nests at the limits to tree growth.

Swallows

Five species of swallows have been recorded for Yosemite, but only three are common. Swallows are often seen swooping and darting agilely as they scoop insects out of the air. They have slender bodies and long pointed wings built for rapid flight. Often nest in colonies.

VIOLET-GREEN SWALLOW *(Tachycineto thalassina)*

Description. White cheeks, flanks, and rump; violet-green back.

Distribution. Breeds from oak woodlands up to subalpine zone.

Remarks. Most common swallow in Yosemite. Does not require open water to forage, but does not avoid water if it is available.

NORTHERN ROUGH-WINGED SWALLOW *(Stelgidopteryx serripennis)*

Description. Brown above, white below.

Distribution. Found from oak woodlands up to ponderosa pine zone. Lower Merced and Tuolumne river canyons.

Remarks. Unlike many other swallows, typically nests in pairs or small groups.

BARN SWALLOW *(Hirundo rustica)*

Description. Deeply forked tail. Reddish brown throat, light under-parts, blue back.

Distribution. Nests from foothills to ponderosa pine zone. Yosemite Valley, Wawona, El Portal, Big Meadow.

Remarks. Tends to hunt over water or wet meadows.

Crows and Jays

Six members of the jay family are known for Yosemite, but only three are common. These birds display exceptional intelligence and use complex vocalizations. Members of this omnivorous group eat a wide variety of foods.

STELLER'S JAY *(Cyanocitta stelleri)*

Description. Blue with black crest and head.
Distribution. Mixed coniferous forests up to red fir zone.
Remarks. Omnivorous. Common in picnic areas. Has complex and varied vocalization. Harsh call.

CLARK'S NUTCRACKER *(Nucifraga columbiana)*

Description. Gray body, black wings, and tail edged with white. Stout bill.
Distribution. Ubiquitous in high country. Associated with pine forests. Tioga Pass, Mount Dana, Tuolumne Meadows.
Remarks. Collects pine seeds from cones, particularly whitebark pine. Caches for later retrieval. May store more than thirty thousand seeds. Most birds seen in Yosemite breed on eastern slope of Sierra.

COMMON RAVEN *(Corvus corax)*

Description. Large, black body. Wedge-shaped tail visible in flight. Stout, black bill.
Distribution. Mainly in foothills, but seen above timberline in summer.
Remarks. With four-foot wingspan, soars like a hawk. Nests on cliffs. Sometimes kills prey, but relies on scavenging. Eats roadkills as well as anything else it can find.

Nuthatches and Chickadees
These small, lively birds are common residents of the forests. All are cavity nesters.

MOUNTAIN CHICKADEE *(Parus gambeli)*

Description. White eyebrow, black cap, light gray sides, gray back. Small and active.
Distribution. Year-round residents range from oak woodlands up to lodgepole pine forest.
Remarks. Most abundant small bird in winter. Forms small flocks. Cavity nester.

RED-BREASTED NUTHATCH (Sitta canadensis)

Description. Red breast and belly, white eyebrow, black cap, gray back. Call sounds like a tiny tin horn.

Distribution. Ponderosa pine zone up to treeline, but most common in white and red fir forests.

Remarks. Eats insects and conifer seeds; caches extra food.

WHITE-BREASTED NUTHATCH (Sitta carolinensis)

Description. Black cap and white face; gray back.

Distribution. Common in oak forests, occasional in ponderosa/Jeffrey pine forests.

Remarks. Often seen foraging under tree bark for insects. Caches acorns for winter food.

Creepers

The only creeper in North America is the brown creeper. It gets its name from its habit of inching up tree boles as it searches for insects.

BROWN CREEPER (Certhia americana)

Description. Head, back, and wings streaked brown; belly white. Small (five to six inches).

Distribution. Old-growth coniferous forests, particularly stands of sequoia and incense cedar. Yosemite Valley, Crane Flat, Mariposa Grove.

Remarks. Unlike nuthatches, which often climb down a tree trunk, brown creeper always goes up a trunk.

Wrens

These small, chunky birds with slender bills often bob their tails up and down or hold them up. Six species are recorded for Yosemite, but only two are relatively common.

ROCK WREN (Salpinctes obsoletus)

Description. Gray-brown back; light colored, finely streaked breast. Six inches long.

Distribution. Rocky areas, talus slopes, cliffs at lower elevations as well as above timberline. Seldom seen in Yosemite Valley. Known from Tuolumne Meadows, Mount Dana, Volgelsang Peak, Merced River canyon.

Remarks. Tolerates very arid conditions.

CANYON WREN (*Catherpes mexicanus*)

Description. Wings barred, back streaked brown, throat white.

Distribution. Cool, shaded canyons with rock outcrops near water, mostly at lower elevations. Yosemite Valley. Merced and Tuolumne river canyons.

Remarks. Hops or creeps while foraging for insects.

Dippers

Only one species of dipper occurs in North America. These distant relatives of wrens have short, stubby bodies and wade underwater in rapid mountain streams.

AMERICAN DIPPER (*Cinclus mexicanus*)

Description. Plump, slate gray body with short wings and tail. Musical, wrenlike song.

Distribution. Along clear, rushing streams to timberline.

Remarks. Bobs up and down when standing; skims low over water when flying. Specialized flaps on nostrils and eyes keep out water. Oil from oil gland waterproofs plumage so birds can forage on stream bottoms. John Muir's favorite bird. Sometimes known as water ousel.

Kinglets

Smallish, active birds that flit among branches of conifers. Often remain all winter in the mountains.

GOLDEN-CROWNED KINGLET (*Regulus satrapa*)

Description. Yellowish crown patch bordered in black; white wing bars, light gray belly, darker back.

Distribution. Common in mixed coniferous forests up to red fir zone.

Remarks. Policy of fire suppression has favored this species, which forages for insects in the tree crowns of dense forests.

RUBY-CROWNED KINGLET *(Regulus calendula)*

Description. Small, plump body; gray back, white wing bars. Male: red stripe on crown.

Distribution. Most common in chaparral, oak woodlands, and riparian forests, except during breeding season when occurs in lodgepole pine or mountain hemlock forests near water. Can be seen in summer at Tioga Pass, Tuolumne Meadows, Glen Aulin.

Remarks. Often hovers as it picks insects off branches.

Thrushes

Eight thrushes have been recorded in Yosemite; the four most common ones are covered here. Some, like the robin, are known by almost everyone. All are good singers.

MOUNTAIN BLUEBIRD *(Sialia currucoides)*

Description. Male: powder blue body with white belly. Female: grayish blue with white belly. Both sexes flash blue rumps when flying.

Distribution. Breeds in red fir/lodgepole pine forest. Prefers open meadows for foraging. Common above timberline. Mount Hoffman, Lyell Fork, Tioga Pass, Tuolumne Meadows.

Remarks. Nests in cavities. Competition for suitable nest holes is fierce.

TOWNSEND'S SOLITAIRE *(Myadestes townsendi)*

Description. Gray body, white eye ring, white outer tail feathers.

Distribution. Breeds from ponderosa pine zone up to lodgepole pine forest. Prefers open stands. Tuolumne Meadows, Mariposa Grove, Crane Flat.

Remarks. Flies from perch and hawks insects from air.

HERMIT THRUSH *(Catharus guttatus)*

Description. Tail and eye ring reddish; back brown; breast buff with darker spots; belly white.

Distribution. Common in mixed coniferous forests up to lodgepole pine zone. Inhabits stands of oaks in winter.

Remarks. Has beautiful flutelike song.

AMERICAN ROBIN *(Turdus migratorius)*

Description. Brown back, red breast, black head.

Distribution. Forest sites from oak woodlands up to lodgepole pine zone. Forages in meadows.

Remarks. Outside the breeding season forms large flocks. One flock in Tuolumne River canyon was estimated to contain one hundred thousand birds.

Starlings

These chunky birds have dark, glossy plumage and often form flocks.

EUROPEAN STARLING *(Sturnus vulgaris)*

Description. Iridescent black plumage; yellow bill in breeding adults.

Distribution. Lower elevation oak woodlands and riparian zones.

Remarks. Introduced from Europe; aggressive cavity nester has displaced many native species by usurping holes.

Vireos

Vireos are small songbirds; some have white wing bars. They are chunkier than warblers. Three species have been recorded for Yosemite; two are common in the park.

SOLITARY VIREO *(Vireo solitarius)*

Description. White eye ring, two white wing bars. Five and one-half inches long.

Distribution. Ponderosa pine/black oak communities and other mixed coniferous forests.

Remarks. Has suffered declines as a result of cowbird parasitism.

WARBLING VIREO *(Vireo gilvus)*

Description. Olive gray back, white underparts, white eye stripe.

Distribution. Wooded sites, particularly riparian sites with willows, alders, and cottonwoods up to red fir forest.

Remarks. Beautiful warbling voice of male gives rise to name. Declining rapidly as a result of nest parasitism by brown-headed cowbirds.

Warblers

These small, perky birds with slender bills live mainly upon insects gleaned from tree branches and needles. Warblers are known for their complex, warbling songs. The ten species known from Yosemite occur in a wide variety of habitats; seven are covered here.

NASHVILLE WARBLER *(Vermivora ruficapilla)*

Description. Bold white eye ring, gray head, olive body, yellow breast and belly.

Distribution. Mid-elevation mixed coniferous forests including black oak/ponderosa pine zone.

Remarks. Forages on broad-leaved shrubs and trees like black oak.

YELLOW WARBLER *(Dendroica petechia)*

Description. Yellow body. Reddish streaks on male breast absent or very pale in female.

Distribution. Dense riparian shrubs, usually near water.

Remarks. Has declined with destruction of riparian habitat from livestock grazing, logging, and dams. Now brown-headed cowbirds also a threat.

YELLOW-RUMPED WARBLER *(Dendroica coronata)*

Description. Rump, patch on throat, and cap yellow; otherwise gray above; white belly.

Distribution. Common at low elevations year-round, but most common during breeding season in mixed coniferous forests up to lodgepole pine zone.

Remarks. This species formerly included two forms that were considered separate species—Audubon's and myrtle warblers.

BLACK-THROATED GRAY WARBLER *(Dendroica nigrescens)*

Description. Gray back, black and white head, white belly.

Distribution. Prefers oak forests or pine forests with oaks. Moves up-slope after nesting. Tuolumne River canyon, Yosemite Valley, El Portal.

Remarks. Specializes in oaks more than any other Sierran warbler.

HERMIT WARBLER *(Dendroica occidentalis)*

Description. Yellow head, dark back, white belly. Male: black chin.

Distribution. Large trees in mixed coniferous forests, especially black oak and ponderosa pine. Yosemite Valley, Tuolumne Grove, Mariposa Grove.

Remarks. Most common warbler in mid-elevation forests.

MACGILLIVRAY'S WARBLER *(Oporornis tolmiei)*

Description. White crescents around eye; gray back, head, and throat; yellow belly.

Distribution. Breeds in shrubs along streams from ponderosa pine zone up to red fir zone.

Remarks. May be found in alpine zone after breeding season.

WILSON'S WARBLER *(Wilsonia pusilla)*

Description. Olive back; yellow face, chest, and belly. Male: black cap.

Distribution. Riparian areas and wet meadows at mid to high elevations.

Remarks. Male sometimes has several mates in one season.

Tanagers

The western tanager is the only representative of this mostly tropical group in the Sierra.

WESTERN TANAGER *(Piranga ludoviciana)*

Description. Male: red head, yellow belly, yellow upper wing bar, black back and tail. Female: greenish above, yellow underneath.

Distribution. Breeds in coniferous forests. Yosemite Valley, Mariposa Grove, Porcupine Flat.

Remarks. Feeds primarily on insects and fruit.

Grosbeak

The name grosbeak means "large beak." These birds have short, stout bills designed for crushing seeds.

BLACK-HEADED GROSBEAK *(Pheucticus melanocephalus)*

Description. Male: large triangular bill, cinnamon underparts, black head. Female: brown, streaked.

Distribution. Oak woodlands, mixed coniferous forests, and riparian areas.

Remarks. Males sing beautifully during breeding season.

Sparrows, Towhees, and Juncos

There are fifteen species in this group in Yosemite. Most of these birds have strong bills for eating seeds; however, insects are important to the diet of young birds. The seven most common park species in this group are covered here.

RUFOUS-SIDED TOWHEE *(Pipilo erythrophthalmus)*

Description. Male: head black, wings black with white barring, sides rufous, belly white.

Distribution. Blue oak savanna to mixed coniferous forests.

Remarks. Gathers insects on forest floor by scratching leaves away.

CHIPPING SPARROW *(Spizella passerina)*

Description. Adult: bright chestnut crown, white eyebrow, black line through eye; otherwise brownish with streaks.

Distribution. Favors dry habitats from chaparral foothills to subalpine lodgepole pine.

Remarks. Often forages on forest floor for insects and seeds.

FOX SPARROW (Passerella iliaca)

Description. Dark brown back; heavily streaked chest with central spot; reddish rump.

Distribution. Chaparral to lodgepole pine zone.

Remarks. Feeds on ground by scratching in litter for insects and seeds.

SONG SPARROW (Melospiza melodia)

Description. Long, rounded tail pumps up and down in flight. Brown on back, whitish sides, streaked breast with large central spot.

Distribution. Most common at low elevations. Breeds in dense vegetation along streams from blue oak savanna up to black oak/ponderosa pine zone.

Remarks. Forages on ground; has beautiful song.

LINCOLN'S SPARROW (Melospiza lincolnii)

Description. Striped breast, brown back, white belly, gray central crown stripe.

Distribution. Wet meadows and streamside thickets to red fir zone.

Remarks. Feeds mainly on seeds and insects on ground.

WHITE-CROWNED SPARROW (Zonotrichia leucophrys)

Description. Black and white striped crown, grayish breast, brown back.

Distribution. Common in willows and young lodgepole pine forests at higher elevations.

Remarks. Birds from different areas sing in different dialects.

DARK-EYED JUNCO (Junco hyemalis)

Description. Black hood, brownish back, gray rump, white outer tail feathers.

Distribution. Very abundant in open forests and meadows from ponderosa pine zone to timberline.

Remarks. Feeds mostly on the ground by foraging for seeds, except
during nesting season when insects constitute the bulk of its diet.

Orioles and Blackbirds

Members of this group occur in a wide variety of habitats and typically
have pointed bills.

BREWER'S BLACKBIRD (Euphagus cyanocephalus)

Description. Male: eyes yellow, head black with purplish glow. Female:
plumage gray-brown.

Distribution. Most common in foothills, but found in young forests
from lowlands to subalpine.

Remarks. Common in campgrounds.

RED-WINGED BLACKBIRD (Agelaius phoeniceus)

Description. Male: black with red shoulder patches. Female: plumage
streaked brown and white.

Distribution. Marshes, cattails, and shrubs by water.

Remarks. Males defend patches of marsh vigorously against intruders.

BROWN-HEADED COWBIRD (Molothrus ater)

Description. Male: brown head and glossy, purple-green body. Female:
brown plumage with streaked breast.

Distribution. Riparian areas and moist meadows up to ponderosa pine
belt.

Remarks. Has spread across the West in the footsteps of human disturbance; often associated with cattle. Practices nest parasitism, planting
eggs in the nests of other birds, who then raise baby cowbirds to the
exclusion of their own. Cowbirds are responsible for major declines in
many warbler, vireo, and other small songbird species.

Finches

Finches have thick bills to assist in cracking seeds—their primary food source. The flight of finches is often undulating. Eleven species of finches occur in Yosemite; only three are common most of the year.

ROSY FINCH (*Leucosticte arctoa*)

Description. Brown back, gray head with black forehead, pinkish rump and belly.

Distribution. Remains year-round above 10,000 feet in the alpine zone; occasionally seen in forest edges.

Remarks. No other bird is so consistently found at higher elevations.

CASSIN'S FINCH (*Carpodacus cassinii*)

Description. Male: crimson crown, pinkish throat, brown streaked back. Female: brown streaked throughout.

Distribution. Open lodgepole pine and mixed coniferous forests.

Remarks. Numbers fluctuate widely from year to year.

Pipits

Pipits are sparrow-sized birds of alpine uplands.

WATER PIPIT (*Anthus spinoletta*)

Description. Brownish gray above, faintly streaked below; white outer feathers on tail.

Distribution. Alpine tundra.

Remarks. Bobs as it walks on ground looking for insects. Only recently discovered as breeder in Yosemite. One nest by Reymann Lake found in July 1992.

MAMMALS

A mammal's fur provides insulation, permitting warm-bloodedness, which in turn allows the animal to remain active year-round and at night. Because most mammals are active after dark and live underground or beneath cover on the forest floor, one is not likely to see many of the species described. Mammals have complex behavior and the ability to learn. All North American mammals bear their young alive.

Species Accounts

The following mammals are recorded for Yosemite National Park or nearby areas and thus thought to occur in Yosemite.

Marsupials

OPOSSUM *(Didelphis virginiana)*

Description. Naked tail, ratlike face, gray body, pouch.

Distribution. Riparian areas at lower elevations.

Remarks. Introduced into California in 1910; impact upon native wildlife unknown. Feeds on lizards, frogs, small snakes, and bird eggs. Young opossums are born blind with poorly developed legs. By instinct, they pull themselves across the mother's abdomen and into the pouch where they begin nursing.

Shrews

Shrews look like small mice, but they have five toes on each front foot instead of four. Few shrews are over three inches long. The eyes are small and weak, but the senses of smell and hearing are keen. Like bats, shrews make rapid twittering squeaks to assist in navigation. These insectivores forage continuously day and night. A shrew consumes its weight in food every three hours. If deprived of food for even a few hours, shrews starve.

The diet consists of crickets, earthworms, ants, and salamanders. Shrews produce a mild poison that subdues their prey. Few shrews live more than one year.

MOUNT LYELL SHREW (*Sorex lyelli*)

Description. Head and body two inches.

Distribution. Known only from alpine areas of the Sierra in and near Yosemite. Favors riparian sites.

Remarks. Named for Mount Lyell in Yosemite, where the species was first discovered.

VAGRANT SHREW (*Sorex vagrans*)

Description. Reddish brown in summer; gray in winter. Tail bicolored; feet dark.

Distribution. Mid- to high elevations in riparian areas.

Remarks. Like most shrews, these animals usually die by their second season. Captive vagrant shrews have eaten one and one-half times their weight in a single day.

DUSKY SHREW (*Sorex monitcolos*)

Description. Brown summer coat; grayer in winter. Belly whitish; tail bicolored. Head and body three inches.

Distribution. Riparian habitats in Jeffrey pine, red fir, and lodgepole pine forests. Rarely far from water.

Remarks. Formerly called montane shrew because of close association with mountain uplands.

ORNATE SHREW (*Sorex ornatus*)

Description. Dull brown with pale belly and bicolored tail.

Distribution. Riparian areas and brushy hillsides at lower elevations in oak to ponderosa pine zones.

Remarks. Feeds on insects and other invertebrates.

WATER SHREW (*Sorex palustris*)

Description. Dark brown-gray body; dense velvety fur. Stiff hairs on hind feet. Large for a shrew; head and body three inches.

Distribution. Waterways, lakes, and streams at higher elevations.

Remarks. Swims and dives like an otter; waterproof fur becomes encapsulated in air bubble. Forages for tadpoles, fish, and invertebrates.

TROWBRIDGE'S SHREW (*Sorex trowbridgii*)

Description. Brown in summer; gray in winter. Tail bicolored. Head and body two and one-half inches.

Distribution. Mixed coniferous forests.

Remarks. Short lived, like all shrews; entire population turns over in a year or so.

Moles

Moles spend their entire lives underground. Their shovel-like front paws dig burrows in soft soil, where they forage for insects and bulbs. Moles have very smooth and fine fur; this allows them to move easily in their tunnels. They have poor eyesight.

BROAD-FOOTED MOLE (*Scapanus latimanus*)

Description. Head and body five to six inches. Light gray; narrow snout with whiskers; short tail; small, weak eyes; shovel-like feet.

Distribution. Forest openings and meadows with loose soils at all elevations.

Remarks. Unlike gophers, prefers moist soils.

Bats

The only mammals that can fly, bats are sometimes referred to as flying mice because of their rodent-like appearance. Bats have taken over the nighttime niche of insect-feeding birds. They navigate by means of echolocation. High-pitched sounds are emitted, and the length of time it takes for a sound to bounce off an object and to return as an echo is used to gauge the object's distance.

Most bats produce only one young annually. After it is born, the young bat clings to its mother's fur, often accompanying her on nighttime forays.

Because of their small body size, bats are vulnerable to excess heat loss. During winter hibernation, bats cluster together to conserve warmth. As an additional heat conservation mechanism, their body temperatures drop to near air temperature. If hibernating bats are disturbed by people, the resulting energy expenditure uses up valuable fat reserves.

Bat numbers are declining throughout North America because of habitat loss (some bats roost in old-growth trees) and poison buildup.

LITTLE BROWN MYOTIS (Myotis lucifugus)

Description. Dark brown with lighter belly; dark face, ears, wings, and feet. Three to four inches long.

Distribution. Widely distributed near water from mid to high elevations.

Remarks. Associated with mountain forests. Hibernates in caves.

YUMA MYOTIS (Myotis yumanensis)

Description. Dull brown or buff on top part of body.

Distribution. Widespread in riparian zones up to ponderosa pine forest. Forages near water.

Remarks. Maternity colonies up to a thousand individuals.

LONG-EARED MYOTIS (Myotis evotis)

Description. Pale golden fur; large black ears.

Distribution. Uncommon inhabitant of forests. Roosts in trees.

Remarks. Emerges after dark. Flies low; eats beetles, moths, and insects taken in flight.

CALIFORNIA MYOTIS (Myotis californicus)

Description. Small buff-colored body; medium-sized, dark ears; dark face.

Distribution. Oak woodlands at low elevations, usually below 5,000 feet.

Remarks. Some individuals live up to fifteen years in the wild. Feeds on beetles and moths.

SMALL-FOOTED MYOTIS (Myotis leibii)

Description. Light golden brown back; black ears and face.
Distribution. Prefers arid uplands.
Remarks. Takes moths, beetles, and other insects. Hibernates in winter.

SILVER-HAIRED BAT (Lasionycteris noctivagans)

Description. Back dark brown or black with white-tipped hairs. Ears short and broad.
Distribution. Forested areas.
Remarks. Uses large, old-growth trees for roosting and breeding. Flies slowly; feeds on moths.

WESTERN PIPISTRELLE (Pipistrellus hesperus)

Description. Yellowish or dull fur; short, dark ears. Small body.
Distribution. Common at lower elevations below ponderosa pine forests.
Remarks. Emerges early in evening, long before dark.

BIG BROWN BAT (Eptesicus fuscus)

Description. Dark ears and wings lack fur; brownish, glossy body fur.
Distribution. Forest openings and meadows except in alpine zone.
Remarks. Feeds twenty to sixty feet above ground.

RED BAT (Lasiurus borealis)

Description. Back reddish, hair tips whitish.
Distribution. Wooded areas at lower elevations. Roosts in moderately dense stands of trees.
Remarks. Flies long before dark; forages on moths and other insects.

HOARY BAT *(Lasiurus cinereus)*

Description. Dark brown with white-tipped body hairs that give a frosted look.
Distribution. Wooded areas with large trees near water.
Remarks. Roosts alone in trees.

SPOTTED BAT *(Euderma maculatum)*

Description. Black body; large ears; three white spots on back.
Distribution. Foothills to ponderosa pine zone.
Remarks. Rare cave dweller.

TOWNSEND'S BIG-EARED BAT *(Plecotus townsendii)*

Description. Light brown fur; long ears; glandular swellings on snout.
Distribution. Widespread in western Sierra Nevada.
Remarks. Requires caves for roosting and hibernation.

PALLID BAT *(Antrozous pallidus)*

Description. Sandy-colored fur; long ears separated at base.
Distribution. Foothill grasslands to mixed coniferous forest zone.
Remarks. Feeds mostly on flightless insects by foraging on the ground.

BRAZILIAN FREE-TAILED BAT *(Tadarida brasiliensis)*

Description. Small, brown, free-tailed bat with dull fur.
Distribution. Chaparral and grasslands at lower elevations.
Remarks. Feeds high in the air, typically more than a hundred feet above the ground. Colonial; forms huge roosting and maternity colonies.

Pikas

These small herbivores look like tiny rabbits with small, round ears and hind legs that are similar in size to their forelegs. They inhabit rocks and talus slopes in mountainous areas.

PIKA *(Ochotona princeps)*

Description. Small gray body, tiny tail. Ears short and round. Voice a loud *Ek-ek!*
Distribution. Rocks and meadows in alpine areas.
Remarks. Hay gathered during summer is dried and stored among boulders for winter use. Does not hibernate; remains active under snow all winter.

Rabbits and Hares

These small herbivores use their large hind limbs for running and jumping. Hares are born fully furred and able to walk immediately. Rabbits are born naked, blind, and helpless.

BRUSH RABBIT *(Sylvilagus bachmani)*

Description. Small rabbit with short legs and somewhat pointed ears.
Distribution. Chaparral, dense brush at lower elevations.
Remarks. Secretive. Eats grasses, forbs, and browse.

DESERT COTTONTAIL *(Sylvilagus audubonii)*

Description. Long-legged cottontail with grayish back and large ears.
Distribution. Chaparral, blue oak savanna, and open mixtures of shrubs and meadows.
Remarks. More likely than brush rabbit to forage in open.

SNOWSHOE HARE *(Lepus americanus)*

Description. Medium-sized hare with short ears and large feet. White in winter; brown in summer.
Distribution. Rare. High elevations of Sierra in lodgepole pine forests.
Remarks. Reaches southern limits in northern Yosemite.

WHITE-TAILED JACKRABBIT *(Lepus townsendii)*

Description. Large hare with conspicuous white tail. Brown in summer; white in winter.

Distribution. Mostly on eastern slope of Sierra, up into the alpine and open subalpine forests.

Remarks. A grassland species that occasionally wanders to high elevations.

BLACK-TAILED JACKRABBIT *(Lepus californicus)*

Description. Black tail, long legs, long ears.

Distribution. Chaparral and open grasslands in arid lands.

Remarks. Typically evades predators by running erratically.

Mountain Beavers

These rabbit-sized nocturnal creatures of old-growth forests are seldom seen and actually are not beavers.

MOUNTAIN BEAVER *(Aplodontia rufa)*

Description. Stocky rodent with small eyes, reduced external ears, and tiny tail; dark brown fur with white spot by each ear. Head and body fourteen to seventeen inches.

Distribution. Riparian habitat with thick undergrowth.

Remarks. Not aquatic despite its name. Eats ferns, as well as thimbleberry, dogwood, and other shrubs.

Chipmunks

These small, active rodents are conspicuously striped. They eat seeds and some insects, such as caterpillars.

ALPINE CHIPMUNK *(Eutamias alpinus)*

Description. Fur yellowish with stripes on head; lateral stripes gray. Head and body four to four and one-half inches.

Distribution. Open coniferous forests, especially lodgepole pine near timberline. Prefers talus slopes near down logs.

Remarks. Hibernates from November through April.

YELLOW PINE CHIPMUNK *(Eutamias amoenus)*

Description. Sides reddish. Dark brown head stripes. Smaller than other forest-dwelling chipmunks; head and body four and one-half to five inches.
Distribution. Ponderosa and Jeffrey pine forests.
Remarks. May not hibernate.

ALLEN'S CHIPMUNK *(Eutamias senex)*

Description. Large body with short ears, dull fur, and grayish light lateral stripes.
Distribution. Streamside thickets in coniferous forests with dense understories.
Remarks. Thought to hibernate in winter.

MERRIAM'S CHIPMUNK *(Eutamias merriami)*

Description. One of the largest chipmunks in California. Dull colored. Grayish light stripes; grayish head.
Distribution. Blue oak savanna to Jeffrey pine zone where understory is shrubby.
Remarks. Eats seeds of chaparral species like manzanita.

LONG-EARED CHIPMUNK *(Eutamias quadrimaculatus)*

Description. Brightly colored with long ears and white patches behind ears; underside of tail reddish.
Distribution. Open, mature ponderosa pine and mixed coniferous forests.
Remarks. Caches food for future use.

LODGEPOLE CHIPMUNK *(Eutamias speciosus)*

Description. Top of head brown; outer dorsal stripes white; sides brownish red. Head and body five inches.
Distribution. Yosemite northward in Jeffrey pine and Lodgepole pine forests.
Remarks. Spends a lot of time in trees. Climbs well.

Ground Squirrels

Ground squirrels are small to medium-sized rodents. Their bodies may be spotted, striped, or flecked, but they lack head stripes. The tail is seldom bushy. Ground squirrels typically live in open places and don't climb trees.

BELDING'S GROUND SQUIRREL (Spermophilus beldingi)

Description. Gray-brown with dark brown back. Short tail sparsely haired but tipped in black. Body eight to nine inches.

Distribution. Subalpine meadows in red fir and lodgepole pine zone where soils are loose and well drained.

Remarks. Known as "picket pin" because of its habit of standing upright when alarmed. Hibernates from September to April.

CALIFORNIA GROUND SQUIRREL (Spermophilus beecheyi)

Description. Looks like a gray tree squirrel, with white dots on back and without bushy tail. Body nine to eleven inches.

Distribution. Prefers dry open slopes among oaks.

Remarks. Lives in colonies. Numbers increase with overgrazing or other disturbance. Will estivate (go into hibernation when conditions become hot and dry) at lower elevations.

GOLDEN-MANTLED GROUND SQUIRREL (Spermophilus lateralis)

Description. Looks like a big chipmunk, but lacks stripes on face. Bright white stripe bounded by black stripes. Head and body six to eight inches.

Distribution. Common in open forests at middle and high elevations and in alpine meadows.

Remarks. Hibernates. Food transported in cheek pouches is cached in burrows.

Marmots

Marmots look like the familiar groundhog, to which they are closely related. Marmots live in rock piles and talus slopes. They are colonial and hibernate all winter.

Yellow-bellied marmots, common in rock piles throughout Yosemite's high country, live in colonies that are usually dominated by a mature male. These rodents hibernate most of the year; during the five months they are active in summer, they must put on enough fat to sustain them through the winter.

YELLOW-BELLIED MARMOT (*Marmota flaviventris*)

Description. Chunky ground squirrel with rusty, grizzled back and yellowish belly. Eyes small; tail bushy. Waddles as it walks. Head and body fourteen to twenty inches.

Distribution. Very common in rocky outcrops near meadows and openings in forests from Jeffrey pine and red fir stands to alpine zone.

Remarks. Often seen basking on rock in sun. Badgers, golden eagles, and coyotes prey on marmots.

Tree Squirrels

There are three species of tree squirrels in Yosemite. The Douglas squirrel and western gray squirrel are abroad in daylight; the flying squirrel is nocturnal and unlikely to be seen. Members of this group have bushy tails and small, erect ears. They are active on the ground and in trees. None hibernate.

WESTERN GRAY SQUIRREL (Sciurus griseus)

Description. Silver-gray, with grizzled fur above; white belly. Head and body nine to twelve inches; bushy tail ten to twelve inches long.
Distribution. Woodlands, from oaks up to Jeffrey pine forests.
Remarks. Acorns of black and blue oak and pine seeds predominate in diet. Caches acorns for future consumption.

DOUGLAS SQUIRREL (Tamiasciurus douglasii)

Description. Brownish back, white chest, bushy tail. Head and body six to seven inches long.
Distribution. Coniferous forests from middle to high elevations.
Remarks. Active; scolds intruders with loud chatter. Eats seeds, mushrooms, and leaf buds. Seeds of conifers are major winter food.

NORTHERN FLYING SQUIRREL (Glaucomys sabrinus)

Description. Brownish gray fur, flattened tail. Membrane stretched between legs creates flap for gliding. Head and body five to six inches.
Distribution. Mature and old-growth coniferous forests.
Remarks. Glides up to one hundred fifty feet. Preyed on by owls. Nocturnal. Searches for food on ground.

Pocket Gophers

These are stocky rodents with very small eyes and ears, external cheek pouches, and naked tails. The yellowish front teeth protrude. Pocket gophers have shovel-like front paws for burrowing. They prefer more arid soils than moles. In winter gophers tunnel under snow; when the snow melts the cores of dirt pushed into these tunnels show where gophers were active.

BOTTA'S POCKET GOPHER (Thomomys bottae)

Description. Dull brown fur. Long front claws for digging. Cheek pockets.

Distribution. Abundant below 5,000 feet in areas with loose soils, especially meadows.

Remarks. Eats bulbs, roots, and stems. Remains underground in tunnels most of the time. Burrowing activities important for turning over and mixing soils.

MOUNTAIN POCKET GOPHER (Thomomys monticola)

Description. Dark brown fur on back and sides; white fur on backs of forefeet; black fur on ears. Head and body five to six inches.

Distribution. Light soils in meadows and open forests from 5,000 feet to alpine zone.

Remarks. Feeds on underground roots, bulbs, and tubers.

Pocket Mice

These rodents are named for their cheek pockets. They are nocturnal, gentle, and seldom seen. Pocket mice stuff their cheek pouches full of food, which they later cache. They are subject to many predators and seldom live more than a year.

CALIFORNIA POCKET MOUSE (Perognathus californicus)

Description. Fur on back includes yellow and black hairs. Head and body three and one-half inches.

Distribution. Prefers arid, brushy locations among chaparral and blue oak savanna.

Remarks. Goes into torpor during cold weather.

Kangaroo Rats

Large eyes, long tails, and large hind legs for jumping characterize kangaroo rats. They occur in arid regions. Like pocket mice, they carry food in fur-lined external cheek pouches. Kangaroo rats produce highly concentrated urine. This allows them to survive without drinking by utilizing the water produced when they metabolize food.

HEERMAN'S KANGAROO RAT (Dipodomys heermanni)

Description. Large, dark-colored body; large eyes, large hind feet, and short upper legs. Tail six to eight inches long with terminal white tuft of fur.

Distribution. Lower elevations; chaparral and oak savanna.

Remarks. Increases in areas where fire or livestock grazing have reduced grass cover.

Mice

These small rodents have long tails, large ears, and large eyes.

WESTERN HARVEST MOUSE (*Reithrodontomys megalotis*)

Description. Delicate brownish mouse with white belly and bicolored tail. Body and head two to three inches.

Distribution. From low elevations up to alpine zone in grassy meadows and brushy areas.

Remarks. Builds a birdlike nest in grass or woodpecker hole.

DEER MOUSE (*Peromyscus maniculatus*)

Description. Small ears. Bicolored (white below, dark above) tail two to five inches long. Body and head three to four inches.

Distribution. Everywhere.

Remarks. Eats fungi as well as seeds and other plant material and insects. Helps control insects that affect forest trees.

BRUSH MOUSE (*Peromyscus boylii*)

Description. Gray-brown back, fulvous sides, white belly; long tail. Head and body about four inches.

Distribution. Shrub understory in oak, ponderosa pine, and mixed conifer zones.

Remarks. Eats insects, seeds, and fungi.

PINYON MOUSE (*Peromyscus truei*)

Description. Ears nearly one inch long. Head and body four inches. Tail short.

Distribution. Open woodlands and brush below ponderosa pine belt.
Remarks. Spends a lot of time in trees and shrubs.

WESTERN JUMPING MOUSE *(Zapus princeps)*

Description. Large hind legs and feet; yellowish sides; dark brown back; very long, bicolored tail; internal cheek pouches.
Distribution. From mixed conifer zone to higher elevations along rivers, streams, lakes, and wet meadows.
Remarks. Feeds on seeds of grasses and flowers. Hops like a kangaroo rat. Hibernates.

Wood Rats

Better known as pack rats, these rat-sized rodents have long tails, naked ears, and large eyes. They build houses of twigs, sticks, and other materials, usually under rock outcrops.

DUSKY-FOOTED WOOD RAT *(Neotoma fuscipes)*

Description. Grayish brown back; white belly; nearly naked, bicolored tail. Head and body eight to nine inches; tail seven to eight inches.
Distribution. Oak woodlands up through mixed coniferous forests. Avoids open grasslands.
Remarks. Stick nests may be six feet tall.

BUSHY-TAILED WOOD RAT *(Neotoma cinerea)*

Description. Tail bushy; white hind feet. Skin gland produces an odor. Body seven to nine and one-half inches; tail five to seven inches.
Distribution. Rock crevices in middle to upper elevation forests of Jeffrey pine, lodgepole pine, and red fir.
Remarks. Active all year. Nests built of huge piles of litter, bones, and twigs.

Voles

This group includes mostly small, mouselike animals with short legs, small eyes, and ears that are partially hidden by fur. The tail is usually short.

HEATHER VOLE *(Phenacomys intermedius)*

Description. Light gray vole with white feet and short, bicolored tail. Head and body three and one-half to four and one-half inches.

Distribution. Alpine meadows and woodlands.

Remarks. Eats bark of twigs and shrubs in winter, seeds and berries in summer. Builds grass nests under snow.

MONTANE VOLE *(Microtus montanus)*

Description. Tail short (one to two inches long) and bicolored; ears small. Grayish brown to blackish fur with whitish belly. Head and body four to five inches.

Distribution. Wet meadows up to 12,000 feet.

Remarks. Does not hibernate.

CALIFORNIA VOLE *(Microtus californicus)*

Description. Grayish brown; tail only faintly bicolored. Head and body about five inches.

Distribution. Below 4,000 feet in grassy locations.

Remarks. Breeds year-round with a population peak every three to four years.

LONG-TAILED VOLE *(Microtus longicaudus)*

Description. Dark gray-brown fur; tail two to three inches and only slightly bicolored. Head and body five inches.

Distribution. Middle to high elevation coniferous forests of lodgepole pine, Jeffrey pine, and red fir.

Remarks. Eats grasses and grasslike plants.

Porcupines

These slow-moving rodents are covered with thick spines.

PORCUPINE *(Erethizon dorsatum)*

Description. Short-legged with small, beady eyes and prominent quills on tail and rump. Body up to twenty-two inches.

Distribution. Throughout the Sierra in coniferous forests.

Remarks. Eats bark off trees. Despite spines, mountain lion and fisher both prey upon porcupine.

Canids

Canids are members of the dog family. The front paws have five toes; hind paws have four.

COYOTE *(Canis latrans)*

Description. Medium-sized dog-like canid with bushy tail; gray or red-dish gray fur; pointed nose.

Distribution. All habitats from foothills up to alpine zone.

Remarks. Eats mice, gophers, rabbits, and almost anything else that comes along.

RED FOX *(Vulpes vulpes)*

Description. Small and slender dog-like animal; fur normally reddish yellow; bushy tail tipped with white; legs and feet black.

Distribution. Middle to upper elevation forests including stands of Jeffrey pine, lodgepole pine, and red fir.

Remarks. Very rare. Eats small rodents, particularly in meadows.

GRAY FOX *(Urocyon cinereoargenteus)*

Description. Could be confused with coyote. Salt-and-pepper fur; bushy, black-tipped tail; rusty-yellowish sides of neck and back of ears.

Distribution. Foothills, chaparral, oak woodlands.

Remarks. Eats fruits, small rodents, rabbits, and birds. Climbs trees.

Bears

There were once two species of bears in Yosemite—grizzly bears and black bears. The last grizzly was killed in Yosemite in 1895; however, the black bear appears to be holding its own.

BLACK BEAR *(Ursus americanus)*

Description. Long snout, small eyes, claws one to one and one-half inches long. Fur varies from black to brown, gray-blue, or even whitish; white spot usually present on chest. Head and body five to six feet.

Distribution. Throughout forested zone of Yosemite. Scraps from back-packers in high country provide new food sources; more bears recently reported above 10,000 feet than in the past.

Remarks. Dens during winter. Can be aroused from dormancy if disturbed.

Raccoons and Their Allies

Raccoons are related to bears. Their posture is plantigrade, that is, they walk on the soles of their feet. Members of this family have alternating dark and light rings on their tails.

RINGTAIL *(Bassariscus astutus)*

Description. Resembles a slender raccoon with large eyes and a very long, bushy, black-and-white-ringed tail.

Distribution. Brushy low-elevation areas, including chaparral and blue oak savanna in foothills.

Remarks. Nocturnal; forages in trees as well as on ground.

RACCOON *(Procyon lotor)*

Description. Black mask over eyes; rings on tail; grayish fur.

Distribution. Riparian areas, mostly at lower elevations.

Remarks. Feeds on crayfish, fish, frogs, and small mammals.

Weasels and Their Allies

Members of this family usually have long, slender bodies, short legs, and scent glands. In the case of skunks, the odor from the scent glands can be very strong.

MARTEN *(Martes americana)*

Description. Dark brown back; yellow-orange throat patch; bushy tail. Head and body sixteen to eighteen inches; tail eight inches.

Distribution. Mixed conifers as well as red fir and lodgepole pine forests.

Remarks. Uses cavities in trees. Feeds on tree squirrels, voles, mice, and berries.

FISHER (*Martes pennanti*)

Description. Dark brown to nearly black fur; long, slender body and bushy tail. Head and body twenty to twenty-five inches.

Distribution. Rare. Primarily in red fir and lodgepole pine forests, although also occurs Jeffrey pine and mixed coniferous forests.

Remarks. Eats squirrels, porcupines, and rabbits. Requires cavities in trees for dens.

ERMINE (*Mustela erminea*)

Description. Dark brown in summer with white belly and feet; white in winter. Head and body six to nine inches.

Distribution. Pine and fir forests at middle to high elevations.

Remarks. Also known as short-tailed weasel. Preys on voles, shrews, and chipmunks. Curious.

LONG-TAILED WEASEL (*Mustela frenata*)

Description. Long, slender body. Fur dark brown with yellowish white underparts in summer; white in winter; tail black-tipped. Head and body nine to ten inches.

Distribution. From foothills to alpine zone. Prefers meadows.

Remarks. Feeds on small mammals such as voles, mice, and chipmunks.

MINK (*Mustela vison*)

Description. Rich, chocolate brown fur; white chin patch. Tail well furred. Head and body thirteen to seventeen inches.

Distribution. Waterways and riparian areas.

Remarks. Excellent swimmer. Feeds on crayfish, fish, frogs, and small mammals.

WOLVERINE (Gulo gulo)

Description. Stocky; looks like a small bear. Dark brown fur; yellowish stripes along sides to rump. Head and body thirty inches.

Distribution. Rare. Subalpine and alpine habitats.

Remarks. Can travel one hundred miles in a week. Usually solitary. Eats carrion and live prey.

BADGER (Taxidea taxus)

Description. Flattened body with short legs; yellowish gray fur and long claws on black feet. White stripe extends from nose over forehead. Head and body eighteen to twenty-two inches.

Distribution. Found throughout the Sierra from foothills to alpine zone; strongly associated with open forests and meadows.

Remarks. Digs out ground squirrels, gophers, and other burrowing animals.

WESTERN SPOTTED SKUNK (Spilogale gracilis)

Description. White spots on forehead and under each ear; four broken, white stripes along neck, back, and sides. Our smallest skunk. Head and body ten to fourteen inches; tail five to nine inches.

Distribution. Foothills up to ponderosa pine zone. Chaparral.

Remarks. Does not hibernate.

STRIPED SKUNK (Mephitis mephitis)

Description. Black body with narrow white stripe on forehead. White stripe on nape divides into a V and continues down back. Head and body fourteen to eighteen inches.

Distribution. Shrubby areas in grasslands, chaparral, and oak woodlands.

Remarks. Feeds on small rodents, insects, carrion, and bird eggs.

RIVER OTTER (Lutra canadensis)

Description. Rich brown color; webbed feet; thick tail; short, stubby legs. Head and body thirty inches; tail fifteen inches.

Distribution. Riparian areas, especially lowland rivers. Recently recorded in high-elevation lakes.

Remarks. Excellent swimmer. Playful. Eats fish.

Felids

Members of the cat family have short, flat faces and retractile claws. These meat eaters hunt by stalking and pouncing on their prey.

MOUNTAIN LION *(Felis concolor)*

Description. Tawny, yellowish brown fur. Weight up to two hundred pounds. Head and body up to five feet long; tail three feet.

Distribution. Throughout the Sierra where deer are found.

Remarks. Feeds mostly on deer, but also adept at capturing porcupines.

BOBCAT *(Felis rufus)*

Description. Short, black-tipped tail. Head and body twenty-five to thirty inches.

Distribution. Shrubby habitat. Chaparral.

Remarks. Feeds on squirrels, mice, and other rodents.

Deer

Deer are hooved mammals with antlers, which are shed each year. In most species only males have antlers.

MULE DEER *(Odocoileus hemionus)*

Description. Coat brown in summer, gray in winter; tail black-tipped. Large, mule-like ears. Antlers branch into equal forks. Reaches four hundred pounds, but usually two hundred pounds or less.

Distribution. Found in all habitats.

Remarks. Migratory; summers at high elevations, winters at low elevations where snow is uncommon.

Sheep

Both sexes of sheep have true horns, which are not shed annually.

BIGHORN SHEEP *(Ovis canadensis)*

Description. Light brown fur; creamy white rump. Rams have massive curled horns; females have smaller, more dagger-like horns. Three feet high at the shoulder.

Distribution. High alpine areas along Sierran crest.

Remarks. Bighorns were once common throughout the Sierra. Overhunting combined with diseases introduced from domestic sheep led to their extirpation in most of the Sierra. The last bighorn disappeared from Yosemite in 1914. They were recently reintroduced into Lee Vining Canyon near Tioga Pass.

ROAD GUIDE

The mileage for each road segment is given from point to point of the drive within Yosemite National Park.

Some of the mileage markers coincide with roadside markers that designate prominent features of the park. For example, T-1 indicates the first roadside marker on the Tioga Road, T-2 is the second marker on the Tioga Road, and so on; V-1 is the first marker on the Yosemite Valley loop road; and B-1 is the first marker on the Big Oak Flat Road. Although some of these markers are noted in this text, not all of them are included. For a complete guide to the park's road marker system, consult the *Yosemite Road Guide* published by the Yosemite Association and available at visitor centers.

Some of the features noted in the text may be visible for a half-mile or more; determining the exact point at which to note the mileage is problematic because there is no official "spot." So if the text suggests, for instance, that at mileage 1.5 there is a meadow, keep in mind that the meadow may be visible for quite some time. Also, sites were noted to the nearest tenth of a mile, rounded up or down; therefore, the mileage numbers are an approximate estimate of distance, not a precise calculation.

The commentary for the valley loop begins by Bridalveil Fall. The Glacier Point commentary begins where this road leaves Highway 41. All others begin where the respective roads enter the park. If, for example, you enter the park at Tioga Pass on Highway 120 from Lee Vining Canyon, the tour would start at the park entrance station in the pass.

Tioga Pass to Crane Flat—Highway 120

This road begins at Highway 395 by Lee Vining on the eastern side of the Sierra Nevada. It is the only access road where visitors can see subalpine forests and even alpine tundra. It traverses glaciated valleys at the head-

waters of the Tuolumne River as well as Tuolumne Meadows, the largest
subalpine meadows in the Sierra Nevada. This road is open only in
summer and early fall.

The first part of the drive on Highway 120 from Highway 395 to Tioga
Pass crosses lands in the Inyo National Forest. A Forest Service ranger
station is located on the south side of the road about 1.2 miles from the
junction with Highway 395. You don't enter Yosemite National Park until
you reach the crest of the range at Tioga Pass. Although the tour will
begin at Tioga Pass, the following description gives a little background on
Lee Vining Canyon.

The climb up Lee Vining Canyon is long and steep. It is not recommended for those towing heavy loads. The start of the road lies at 6,781
feet; the pass is 9,945 feet above sea level.

The highway follows Lee Vining Canyon, which was heavily glaciated
during the last major ice age. As you drive up the canyon, you cross
several glacial moraines. The low, sage-covered hills that border the lower
ends of the canyons are lateral moraines of the Lee Vining Glacier. The
canyon is named for Leroy Vining, an early gold miner and sawmill
operator. Vining built a sawmill in the canyon and sold the lumber to
mining camps in Aurora, Nevada.

Approximately six to eight miles up the canyon, one can look south to
the Dana Plateau in the Ansel Adams Wilderness. Glacial cirques suggesting the carvings of an ice cream scoop are clearly visible in the rugged
mountain across the canyon. About eight miles up the road Warren
Creek comes in from the north. The elevation here is 8,995 feet. About a
mile farther, the road passes Ellery Lake. The lake was named for Nat
Ellery, a road engineer who helped to build the original Tioga Road from
Mono Lake.

As you approach Ellery Lake you cross a major change in rock types.
The lighter rock is granodiorite, a kind of granite that was intruded in
older metasedimentary rocks. These darker, rust-colored rocks were once
part of the floor of an ancient sea. Similar metamorphosed sedimentary
rocks lie along the eastern edge of Yosemite Park and are found in Mount
Dana, the second highest peak in the park.

On the north you pass a side road to Saddlebag Lake, a favorite camping
and fishing area. Saddlebag Lake is also a trailhead for the Hoover
Wilderness, which borders Yosemite National Park on the northeast.

Just past Tioga Lake, which has an Inyo National Forest campground on its north side, lies the old site of Bennettville, a small boom town that served mines operating in the area between 1860 and 1900.

0.0 Tioga Pass. 9,945 feet. Begin road guide at T-39.

Tioga Pass is the highest pass in the Sierra Nevada crossed by an auto road. Tioga is an Iroquois word meaning "where it forks." The Iroquois lived in New York state, and several towns and counties in that region bear this name. It was transferred to the Yosemite area when miners applied it to the town of Bennettville and operated a post office under that name between 1882 and 1884.

The area around Tioga Pass is a mixture of open meadows and lodgepole pine forest. Lodgepole pine has needles in bundles of two and is a common species in Yosemite's high country between 8,000 and 10,000 feet.

The small bodies of water south of the road are locally called the Tioga Tarns. More properly termed kettles, these were formed when ice that had been left by the retreating glaciers was buried in glacial till and subsequently melted.

South of the Tioga Pass Entrance Station lies Mount Dana. At 13,051 feet, it is second highest peak in Yosemite Park. The top of Mount Dana stuck up above the ice sheets that covered much of the Yosemite high country at the height of the last ice age. As a consequence, the summit of Mount Dana remains relatively flat today.

Mount Dana to the south and Mount Gaylor to the north of Tioga Pass are part of the eastern metamorphic belt. Metamorphic volcanic rocks near the top of Mount Dana have an age of 118 million years **(0.2 miles to next point).**

T-38. Dana Meadows.

This area was once covered by the Tuolumne Glacier, the largest glacier in the Sierra Nevada, which flowed downstream for more than sixty-six miles **(0.3 miles to next point).**

Half a mile from Tioga Pass tree trunks and other debris lie scattered on the ground. These are the remains of an avalanche that poured off the mountain to the left and spilled out into the Tioga Tarns area **(0.5 miles to next point).**

To the south of the road, you can see where young lodgepole pines are invading the Tioga Tarns area (0.5 miles to next point).

Mono Pass trailhead parking lot. The road enters a pure lodgepole pine forest (0.3 miles to next point).

Vista pond pullout for view of Mount Dana and Mount Gibbs. Dark color of mountains reflects their metamorphic and volcanic origins (0.8 miles to next point).

T-36. Pullout next to Dana Fork of Tuolumne River. Views of Mounts Dana and Gibbs. Mount Dana and the Dana Fork were named in 1863 by the Whitney Geological Survey party for James Dana, a geology professor at Yale University. Mount Gibbs was named for a Harvard geology professor by Frederick Olmsted.
     The roadcut opposite the pullout reveals a glacial moraine. You can see the unsorted boulders mixed in with gravels (0.2 miles to next point).

Just beyond the pullout are views to the west of Cathedral Peak in the Cathedral Range as well as Coxcomb Peak and Mount Johnson. Cathedral Peak is a good example of a glaciated matterhorn. Such peaks, named for the famous Swiss mountain, were formed when glaciers carved three or four sides of a mountain to create a pointed summit. Cathedral Peak was named by the Whitney Survey in 1863. It was first climbed by John Muir in 1869. Mount Johnson was the center of an ancient volcano (2.7 miles to next point).

Another roadcut through a glacial moraine (0.6 miles to next point).

View of Cathedral Peak just before turn for Tuolumne Lodge (0.5 miles to next point).

Turnoff for wilderness permit parking lot (0.5 miles to next point).

T-31. Cross bridge over Tuolumne River. The name Tuolumne refers to a group of Indians who used to live along the river's banks at low elevations (0.1 miles to next point).

Tuolumne Meadows campground (**0.3 miles to next point**).

Just beyond the gas station, on the right side of the road, a good example of lodgepole pine invading a meadow can be seen. Studies have shown that most lodgepole pine invasions were precipitated by domestic livestock grazing. Although sheep were banned from the park when it was created in 1890, grazing had already disturbed the soils and hydrology in ways that favor pine invasion (**1.2 miles to next point**).

Trailhead for Cathedral Peak (**0.3 miles to next point**).

The road has been skirting Tuolumne Meadows, the largest subalpine meadow area in the entire Sierra Nevada. It was here that John Muir and magazine editor Robert Underwood Johnson camped in 1889. Domestic sheep had just ravaged the meadows. The damage prompted Johnson to urge Muir to propose the creation of Yosemite National Park as a means of protecting Tuolumne Meadows and their watershed. The next year, Muir published two pieces in *Century Magazine* outlining the idea for Yosemite National Park. In the fall of 1890 Congress passed a bill that basically followed Muir's proposal and established Yosemite National Park (**2.4 miles to next point**).

Mountain hemlock on the north side of the road. This species typically grows on cool slopes. It can be identified by its droopy top and green-blue needles. Hemlock reaches the southern limit of its natural range in Yosemite. This is one of the few places you can see this species in the park (**2.1 miles to next point**).

East end of Tenaya Lake. Tenaya Lake is named for Chief Tenaya of the Awhaneeche tribe, who lived in Yosemite Valley at the time of its discovery by whites (**1.3 miles to next point**).

Parking lot to Sunrise Trail (**1.4 miles to next point**).

T-25. Marker identifying Tenaya Lake. Located 8,149 feet above sea level, it is one of the largest natural lakes in Yosemite (**1.0 miles to next point**). T-24. Olmsted Point and overlook. Here one gets a terrific view of Tenaya Lake, Half Dome, and Clouds Rest. Olmsted Point is named for Frederick

Law Olmsted, first chair of the Yosemite Park Commission and designer of Central Park (**1.4 miles to next point**).

T-23. Good view to the south of Clouds Rest cliff face, a 9,926-foot peak along Tenaya Creek. The red-barked trees in this region are red fir. Stands of red fir are often called snow forest because they grow at the elevation with the greatest annual snowfall (**0.4 miles to next point**).

T-22. The road cuts through a glacial moraine here. Red fir is abundant on both sides of the road (**0.4 miles to next point**).

T-21. Turn right for May Lake trailhead. Mount Hoffman can be reached via the May Lake Trail. The views from the top provide a panorama of the entire park (**0.6 miles to next point**).

Nice straightaway with red fir on both sides (**0.6 miles to next point**).

T-20. View of Half Dome (**0.8 miles to next point**).

T-19. Trail to North Dome. Just beyond this pullout is a fine example of red fir forest (**0.5 miles to next point**).

T-18. Short nature trail that identifies common Sierra trees (**0.6 miles to next point**).

T-17. Turnout for Porcupine Flat campground (**1.1 miles to next point**).

Red fir forest with ponderosa pine on drier sites (**0.9 miles to next point**).

Turnout looking over Yosemite Creek. Good views throughout this stretch (**0.9 miles to next point**).

Ponderosa pine and western juniper on drier slopes. Lodgepole pine and red fir on wetter sites (**0.7 miles to next point**).

T-16 Aspen interpretive sign. Aspen is one of the few deciduous species found in the high elevation coniferous forests (**0.4 miles to next point**).

T-15. Yosemite Creek. Just beyond this point are good examples of exfoliation in granite **(1.3 miles to next point).**

T-14. Exfoliating granite. These rocks were formed under great pressure deep in the earth. When they were exposed at the surface the decrease in pressure caused the outer layer of rock to peel off **(0.3 miles to next point).**

T-12. Western juniper interpretive sign. Western juniper can live a thousand years. It is relatively common on rocky ridges in the subalpine forest zone **(1.4 miles to next point).**

T-11. View of Clark Range, named for Galen Clark, the first guardian of Yosemite. Clark built the first hotel at Wawona. He is credited with discovering the Mariposa Grove of sequoia **(2.1 miles to next point).**

Turnoff for T-9 and White Wolf campground **(0.9 miles to next point).**

T-8. Siesta Lake on left. The lake was formed by a terminal moraine from a glacier **(1.4 miles to next point).**

Sign for 8,000-foot elevation **(1.6 miles to next point).**

T-7. Red fir forest **(3.1 miles to next point).**

T-5. South Fork of the Tuolumne River **(1.2 miles to next point).**

Enter burn area on left side of road **(2.4 miles to next point).**

Tamarack Flat, named for lodgepole pine. Early Sierra Nevada residents noted that lodgepole grows in wet habitats, similar to those of eastern tamarack, and dubbed it "tamarack pine" **(0.6 miles to next point).**

Sign for 7,000-foot elevation **(1.7 miles to next point).**

Crane Meadow. Named for sandhill cranes that once foraged here **(0.5 miles to next point).**

Stop sign. Junction with Big Oak Flat Road.

Big Oak Flat Road from Park Entrance to Yosemite Valley Loop Road

Big Oak Flat Road takes its name from the town of Big Oak Flat to the west of the park border. Big Oak Flat was originally a mining community. During the California gold rush of the mid-1800s it boasted a population of three thousand residents. A toll road, the valley's second, was completed in 1874. Part of the old road can still be glimpsed along the one-way road through the Tuolumne sequoia grove, which begins near Crane Flat.

0.0 Entrance to Yosemite on Big Oak Flat Road **(0.7 miles to next point).**

Big Oak Flat Entrance Station. The mixed coniferous forests in this area contain incense cedar, white fir, western white pine, ponderosa pine, and a deciduous species, black oak **(2.2 miles to next point).**

Good views to the north of snowy peaks in the Emigrant Wilderness. From this vantage point, it's easy to see the gently sloping peneplain of the Sierran block **(1.9 miles to next point).**

Trail to Merced sequoia grove. This is the smallest of the park's three sequoia groves. It is a four-mile round trip; the second mile is steep **(2.4 miles to next point).**

The horizonal banding of these reddish metamorphic sedimentary rocks indicates their sedimentary origins **(0.3 miles to next point).**

Light horizontal layers have been tilted up at an angle revealing the way in which the mountains have been uplifted and distorted here **(0.4 miles to next point).**

Entrance to Crane Flat fire lookout **(0.1 miles to next point).**

Crane Flat, 6,800 feet **(0.4 miles to next point).**

Turnoff for Highway 120 east to Tioga Pass and Tuolumne Meadows **(1.2 miles to next point).**

Granitic rock evident on either side of road **(0.9 miles to next point)**.

Nice view of Big Meadow to the south (right) **(0.2 miles to next point)**.

B-6. Big Meadow Overlook. Big Meadow is a former lake that gradually silted in. Trees are now invading the meadow. Much of the grain and hay fed to park horses was once grown here. Today this is an important foraging area for the great gray owl, a rare species in the Sierra.

Across from the parking lot an example of spheroidal weathering around cornerstones can be seen. This reflects the original jointing pattern along horizontal and vertical planes. Weathering takes place along both joints, resulting in a rounded sphere.

Above the outcrop is a patch of manzanita, a twisted, red-barked shrub with evergreen leaves. Large ponderosa pines and incense cedars dominate the forest here **(0.3 miles to next point)**.

Beautiful sugar pines visible **(1.4 miles to next point)**.

Big granite outcrops with white-colored quartz dikes **(0.2 miles to next point)**.

Charred snags from the 1990 burn. If you look at the black oak crowns, you will see sprouts. Studies have shown that black oak in Yosemite Valley has declined by 90 percent because of fire suppression. Here fire burned on both sides of the road, showing how ineffective a fire break is if conditions are extreme. Bulldozing fire lines seldom makes a difference except for fires that are likely to go out anyway **(1.3 miles to next point)**.

Sign for 5,000-foot elevation **(0.6 miles to next point)**.

Road on right to Foresta. Once a resort area, the private lands here have been subdivided. Many of the homes burned in the 1990 fire **(0.6 miles to next point)**.

Tunnel entrance **(0.4 miles to next point)**.

Tunnel exit **(0.1 miles to next point)**.

View of Merced River canyon. Look downstream to see V-shaped river canyon created primarily by water erosion; the U-shaped canyon upstream was sculpted by glaciers (**0.4 miles to next point**).

Tamarack Creek. Early visitors called the lodgepole pine common in the Yosemite high country "tamarack" because of its use of habitat similar to the eastern tamarack (**0.1 miles to next point**).

Cascade Creek. John Muir wrote, "Never was a stream more fittingly named, for as far as I have traced it above and below our camp it is one continuous bouncing, dancing, white bloom of cascades."

The south-facing slopes here are covered with canyon live oaks and a few ponderosa pines (**1.8 miles to next point**).

Stop sign on Highway 140, which heads west to El Portal or east into the Yosemite Valley.

Yosemite Valley Loop Road

The Yosemite Valley is a product of many geological events. Rockfalls along joints, which were later swept away by water, helped to create much of the canyon. Subsequent glaciers extended well beyond the valley toward El Portal; these deepened and smoothed some of the canyon wall and created a U-shaped valley. The valley was once occupied by Indians who depended upon acorns from the many oaks that once dotted the canyon floor. Discovered by whites in 1851, the valley floor was protected in 1864 as Yosemite State Park. In 1905 it was transferred back to the federal government and became part of Yosemite National Park.

0.0 Begin loop road at intersection of one-way road in valley below Bridalveil Fall (**0.3 miles to next point**).

Near the start of the one-way road there is parking on either side for a view of Bridalveil Fall as well as El Capitan, which can be seen to the north. The meadow has a good example of black oak woodland. Black oak was more abundant in the Yosemite Valley when fires were common. It has the ability to sprout from its root crown if a fire kills its above-ground parts (**0.2 miles to next point**).

The road follows the Merced River, which lies to its left. The Merced was named in September 1806 by Gabriel Moraga, a Spanish explorer who called the stream El Rio de Nuestra Señora de la Merced. By the 1850s the name had been shortened to Merced River **(1.0 mile to next point).**

Intersection with crossover circle. If you go all the way to Yosemite Village and begin to leave the valley, you can return to the village via this road **(0.1 miles to the next point).**

Cathedral Picnic area **(0.3 miles to next point).**

V-17. Marker that describes naming and history of Merced River. The Merced headwaters lie at more than 11,000 feet in the Cathedral Range. During the last ice age, glaciers moved down the river valley several times, widening and deepening it **(1.2 miles to next point).**

Yellow Pines and Sentinel Beach turnoff on left **(0.1 miles to next point).**

Pullout for Four Mile Trail and V-18. Sentinel Rock, which was named by the Whitney Survey for its supposed likeness to a watchtower, is south of the road. The cliff rises more than 3,000 feet above the valley floor. At one time Lower Yosemite Village was located here and included Camp Ahwahnee and Leidig's Hotel. The site has since been abandoned and reclaimed. The Four Mile Trail was originally built as a toll trail. It gains 3,200 feet in elevation and ends at Glacier Point, one of the most spectacular viewpoints in the park **(0.4 miles to next point).**

Pullout on left with first good view of Yosemite Falls. The several segments of the falls cascade 2,425 feet; some claim they are the third highest falls in the world. The meadow you are looking across is undergoing restoration. In the early years of the park, cattle were allowed to graze in the valley's meadows, and with the coming of the automobile, it was a common practice to drive out and camp on them as well. Considering the amount of abuse they have suffered, it's surprising there are any meadows left at all **(0.5 miles to next point).**

V-20. Old village location. A store, post office, church, park headquarters, hotel, saloons, and other buildings formerly stood on this spot. They were eventually moved to their present locations on the north side of the valley, where they take advantage of the greater sunshine and warmth. This demonstrates what the entire valley could look like if plans for relocating facilities outside of the park were implemented (0.1 miles to next point).

Intersection with shortcut to Yosemite Village. If you turn left here you cross the Merced River. A lovely view of Half Dome is visible looking upstream from the bridge. For tour, continue straight ahead on one-way road (0.6 miles to next point).

V-21. Leconte Memorial. Joseph LeConte was a famous geologist at the University of California, Berkeley, and one of the people who first supported John Muir's views on the Sierra's glacial history (0.3 miles to next point).

Stop sign and intersection. Turn right for Curry Village; go straight to reach Upper Pines, Lower Pines, and North Pines campgrounds as well as day-use parking lot. Turn left and proceed across Merced River to reach Yosemite Village, Yosemite Lodge, Ahwahnee Hotel, and Lower or Upper River campgrounds. To continue tour turn left (0.1 miles to next point).

Cross Merced River (0.1 miles to next point).

Lower and Upper River campgrounds (0.4 miles to next point).

Meadows on either side of road before village. Most of the trees that are visible are large, old-growth ponderosa pines (0.1 miles to next point).

Turn here for store, clinic, and Ahwahnee Hotel (0.5 miles to next point).

V-2. Pullout next to meadow. Many of the meadows in the park were maintained by frequent fires that removed small invading trees. Early photos of the valley show that it was once more open. Today this is a good place to see black oaks in meadows as well as views of Yosemite Falls, Half Dome, and Royal Arches (0.2 miles to next point).

Road crosses Yosemite Creek. *Yosemite* is a corruption of the supposed Indian name for grizzly bear; however, some evidence suggests the word Yosemite did not exist in native languages. In any event, the first whites to enter the valley wanted to name it in honor of its recent inhabitants and chose the name Yosemite thinking that was the tribe's name for itself **(0.6 miles to next point).**

On the right-hand side is Sunnyside campground, which is frequently used by climbers who come to scale Yosemite's cliffs **(0.3 miles to next point).**

V-6. Rocky Point rock slide. A major slide took place in 1987, when an estimated six hundred thousand cubic yards of rock fell from the nearby cliffs **(1.5 miles to next point).**

View of Sentinel Rock and a large meadow on left rimmed by ponderosa pines and black oak **(0.1 miles to next point).**

Parking lot for El Capitan **(0.3 miles to next point).**

Turnoff to go back toward Yosemite Valley **(0.1 miles to next point).**

El Capitan meadow. Many people come to watch climbers on the face of El Capitan. There is also a nice black oak woodland in the meadow **(0.2 miles to next point).**

V-8. View across valley of Cathedral Rocks; El Capitan visible to the north **(0.5 miles to next point).**

V-9. Lying below El Capitan, this point marks a recessional moraine left by the last glacier to occupy Yosemite Valley. Moraines in the valley acted like dams; here they created the lake that was responsible for the nearly flat valley floor **(0.1 miles to next point).**

On the north side of road is another area that was burned to reintroduce fire into the valley **(0.2 miles to next point).**

V-10. Outwash area for glacier that filled the valley and made it marshy.

Galen Clark, first guardian of Yosemite, dynamited the moraine that blocked the Merced River's flow; this accelerated channel downcutting. Bridalveil Fall can be seen dropping 620 feet (**1.0 miles to next point**).

Attractive black oak woodland frames Cathedral Rocks, which can be seen to the south across the valley (**0.4 miles to next point**).

Junction for road loop back to valley or the road to Wawona.

Those continuing on loop road of valley turn left (south) to cross the Merced River or continue going straight to reach the Big Oak Flat or El Portal entrance roads.

South Entrance on Wawona Road to Turnoff for Glacier Point Road— Highway 41

This route follows the trail used by the Mariposa Battalion in 1851 in their campaign against the Indians of Yosemite. Galen Clark located a cabin and eventually built a hotel along this route to serve tourists coming from the Central Valley. The road was first completed in 1875 and has been improved several times since then. This segment of the road guide begins at the South Entrance and describes the highway from there to the Glacier Point Road turnoff, where you can continue on toward the Yosemite Valley Loop Road or take an excursion to Glacier Point. If you wish to visit the Mariposa sequoia grove, turn right after passing the entrance station; otherwise proceed north (left).

0.0 From the South Entrance Station, the road winds through a mixed coniferous forest of sugar pine, white fir, black oak, and incense cedar (**1.2 miles to next point**).

White alder, a common riparian species with smooth, gray bark, is seen along the little creek crossed by the road (**0.1 miles to next point**).

Shortly after crossing the creek, you pass a couple of large ponderosa pines, which can be identified by their reddish yellow bark and long needles in bundles of three. As you descend in elevation toward the South Fork of the Merced River you will begin to see more ponderosa pines because conditions are drier and warmer at lower elevations **(3.1 miles to next point).**

Off to left are some meadows and the Wawona golf course. This portion was not added to the park until 1932. It is the area where Galen Clark located his cabin and later his hotel. *Wawona* is supposedly an Indian word meaning "big tree." The large trees surrounding the Wawona Hotel are primarily ponderosa pines **(0.3 miles to next point).**

W-10. Turnoff for Pioneer Yosemite Historic Center, which includes an old jail, cabins, a covered bridge, and other equipment from the early days of Yosemite **(0.05 miles to next point).**

W-9. Cross the South Fork of the Merced River, which has its headwaters on the park's southern border **(0.1 miles to next point).**

Road on right to Wawona Ranger Station **(0.6 miles to next point).**

Picnic area along South Fork of the Merced River **(0.25 miles to next point).**

W-8. Wawona campground. This was the site of the first park headquarters when the U.S. Army had jurisdiction over Yosemite. From this point the road leaves the South Fork of the Merced River and climbs toward Glacier Point Road **(3.4 miles to next point).**

Mosquito Creek sign. Pacific dogwood, a flowering tree with beautiful white blossoms in spring, is abundant along the creek **(0.3 miles to next point).**

Sign for 5,000-foot elevation **(0.1 miles to next point).**

Alder Creek sign. Alder Creek, named for the surrounding abundance of alders, is a tributary of the South Fork of the Merced River. It is thought that the Whitney Survey named the creek during its 1863 expedition to Yosemite **(3.3 miles to next point).**

Bishop Creek, named for Samuel Bishop, first sergeant in the Mariposa

Battalion, which "discovered" Yosemite. The town of Bishop in the Owens Valley is also named for this man **(2.2 miles to next point)**.

Rail Creek. Named for Rail Meadow, where trees were cut to produce split rail fences **(0.5 miles to next point)**.

Along this portion of the road you cross outcrops of granitic rock **(0.4 miles to next point)**.

Sign for 6,000-foot elevation. Road climbs to cross Henness Ridge **(0.4 miles to next point)**.

Sign for Yosemite West, a private development on the borders of the park **(0.6 miles to next point)**.

Turn east (right if coming from Wawona) to begin Glacier Point Road. Continue straight if going to Yosemite Valley.

Glacier Point Road

This segment describes the road to Glacier Point and the Bridalveil Creek campground. In winter the road is open only as far as Badger Pass ski area, and chains are sometimes required. Check before proceeding. The view at Glacier Point is one of the most dramatic in the park of those that are accessible by car.

G-1, G-2, G-3, etc., refer to the Glacier Point road markers described in the *Yosemite Road Guide* available from Yosemite Association.

0.0 Stop sign at the beginning of Glacier Point Road **(1.1 miles to next point)**.

The road goes through dense stands of white fir on the shaded north slope. A few pines are mixed in, but most of the trees seen are white fir, a shade-tolerant species that has increased dramatically throughout the Sierra Nevada due to fire suppression **(0.6 miles to next point)**.

Pullout on left-hand side. Good view into Merced River canyon. The canyon is the result of water erosion. You can also see the 1990 burn across the canyon **(0.1 miles to next point)**.

G-1. A view of the Merced River canyon. Sugar pines grow at this pullout **(0.1 miles to next point).**

You pass through an area of burnt snags from the 1990 fire. Fire is an essential element of the Sierran forest, and the snags here represent what you would expect to see in a healthy forest where fire is a natural ecological component **(0.6 miles to next point).**

The white firs on the right side of the road have green lichens covering their trunks to within eight feet of the ground. Because the lichens cannot survive buried for months under the snow, this indicates the average snow depth for this area in winter **(0.6 miles to next point).**

Red fir forest. This red-barked tree grows in what is often called the snow forest because it occurs at the elevation of greatest annual snowfall **(0.4 miles to next point).**

You are now driving through an almost pure red fir forest **(1.4 miles to next point).**

G-2. Road on right is for Badger Pass Ski Area. Badger Pass was built in the 1930s when the goal of the National Park Service was to attract as many people as possible to Yosemite. Today, the operation of a downhill ski area within a national park is of questionable benefit and certainly not in keeping with the purpose of promoting natural features and processes. There is still lots of red fir in this area **(2.3 miles to next point).**

G-3. View of Merced Peak and the Clark Range, named for Galen Clark. The straight road enters lodgepole pine forest, leaving red fir behind. Lodgepole pine has two needles and small, round cones. It tends to be found in the subalpine reaches of Yosemite intermixed with red fir. This pine grows in microhabitats that are either too wet or too dry for red fir **(0.4 miles to next point).**

G-4. Bridalveil Creek campground lies at an elevation of 7,000 feet. There are meadows with glacial erratics on the south (right-hand) side of the road. Erratics are boulders dropped as a glacier retreats. The meadows are being invaded by lodgepole pine here **(0.5 miles to next point).**

G-5. Bridalveil Creek. This creek eventually pours off the lip of Yosemite Valley, forming one of the more spectacular falls in the valley **(0.4 miles to next point).**

On the north (left-hand) side of the road, there are stands of dead lodgepole pines that were killed by a fire. These dead trees are ecologically valuable. They provide snags for cavity-nesting birds to live in, down logs for small mammals to hide under, and wood for beetles and other insects to eat. Such dead trees are one sign of a healthy forest **(0.5 miles to next point).**

Ostrander Lake Trail parking lot. Harvey Ostrander was a sheepman who had a cabin near Bridalveil Creek **(0.5 miles to next point).**

Here you leave the lodgepole pine forest behind and enter red fir forest again **(0.7 miles to next point).**

Trailhead for Mono Meadow Trail. Mono Meadow is named for the Mono tribe that lived on the eastern side of the mountains near Mono Lake. This group regularly crossed the Sierra to trade goods with tribes that lived on the west slope **(0.3 miles to next point).**

Pullout on side of road with good views of Mount Starr King (a dome-shaped mountain with an elevation of 9,092 feet) and the Clark Range. One can see the snags left by a fire that burned the slopes of Mount Starr King. Thomas Starr King was a preacher who visited Yosemite in the 1860s and promoted its wonders. To the south one can also see Horse Ridge and Buena Vista Crest. *Buena vista* is Spanish for "beautiful view." At this point, one can also see Jeffrey pines growing on either side of the road. This pine, which looks a lot like ponderosa pine but has larger cones, replaces ponderosa pine at higher elevations **(0.3 miles to next point).**

G-6. A pullout permits a leisurely view of the Clark Range across Illilouette Creek, which flows north into the Merced River **(2.0 miles to next point).**

G-7. Potholes Meadows **(0.7 miles to next point).**

Open granite slopes with good examples of exfoliation, the peeling away of layers of granite, which is responsible for many of the dome-shaped surfaces in the park (**0.2 miles to next point**).

G-9. Road begins to descend toward Glacier Point (**1.1 miles to next point**).

G-10. Washburn Point vista and parking lot with spectacular views. Jeffrey pines frame Half Dome. You can see Mount Conness (12,590 feet) up Tenaya Creek. Closer in are North Dome, Liberty Cap, and Nevada Falls. To the southeast and south are the Clark Range and Buena Vista Crest (**0.8 miles to next point**).

G-11. Glacier Point parking lot. Glacier Point lies at 7,214 feet and provides a panoramic view of the upper Merced River valley. From its summit, cliffs drop 3,000 feet into the valley below.

Highway 41 from Glacier Point Road to Yosemite Valley

This section of the road guide describes the highway between the junctions with Glacier Point Road and the Yosemite Valley Loop Road. This stretch of road descends into Yosemite Valley, providing some spectacular views.

0.0 Junction of Glacier Point Road and main road to Yosemite Valley. The road descends toward Yosemite Valley heading in a generally northeast direction (**1.7 miles to next point**).

Pullout on left. In 1990, fires burned these trees. Some large incense cedars and ponderosa pines survived, but white fir trees in understory were killed by the blaze (**0.1 miles to next point**).

Road crosses Avalanche Creek. Probably named by the Whitney Survey in the 1860s (**0.1 miles to next point**).

Pulloff with view of Merced River canyon (**1.5 miles to next point**).

Road crosses Grouse Creek. There are dozens of "Grouse" creeks, lakes, meadows, and other place names in the Sierra. Most are named for the blue grouse, a chickenlike bird common in the mixed coniferous forests of the western slope (2.5 miles to next point).

Pullout on north side of road with first view of Yosemite Valley. El Capitan and Half Dome are also visible. You can see the U-shaped valley that was carved and steepened by glacial ice. Across from the parking area, the results of exfoliation, or the peeling away of granite, are visible. Most of the vegetation surrounding the pullout is dominated by ponderosa pine, incense cedar, canyon oak, and manzanita. Across the Merced River canyon you can see the road to Big Oak Flat. Most of the slopes across the canyon are covered with canyon oak, but higher up pine begins to dominate (0.3 miles to next point).

The road passes through a forest with some Douglas-fir as well as bigleaf maple. Both species are more common farther north in the Pacific Northwest and reach their southern limits in the Sierra Nevada. They prefer cool, moist locations (0.5 miles to next point).

Enter Wanona tunnel. Built in 1933, it is 0.8 miles in length and the longest tunnel in the park (0.8 miles to next point).

W-2. Parking lot after tunnel. Great view of El Capitan, Bridalveil Fall, and Half Dome. You can see the lake bed that once filled the valley, represented by the flat valley floor and glacially carved, steep-sided canyon. Ponderosa pine, incense cedar, and Douglas-fir are the dominant trees found at the viewpoint (1.5 miles to next point).

W-1. Bridalveil Fall parking lot. Trail to base of the falls. The 620-foot falls pours from the hanging valley, a side canyon carved by tributary glaciers of main trunk valley glaciers (0.1 miles to next point).

End of Highway 41. Enter Yosemite Valley Loop Road.

Merced Road or the El Portal Entrance to Yosemite—Highway 140

This stretch of Highway 140 follows the Merced River, eventually joining the Yosemite Valley Loop Road. This road was once the only year-round access to the park. Today, however, two other highways are also kept open in winter. This is the lowest and hottest part of the park. Many species of plants and animals not found anywhere else in Yosemite may be encountered along this road.

0.0 Park boundary. The border lies approximately one mile beyond *El Portal*, a Spanish word meaning "gateway." This small community lies at 1,900 feet. El Portal was the original railway head for the Yosemite Valley Railroad Company, which reached Yosemite in 1907 **(1.1 miles to next point).**

As you drive along the Merced River, you are treated to an excellent example of a V-shaped, water-carved river canyon, unlike the broader U-shaped, glacier-carved canyon upstream. Canyon oak is abundant here **(1.0 mile to next point).**

Arch Rock Entrance Station. Huge boulders arch over the roadway, creating a natural tunnel **(2.9 miles to next point).**

Road crosses Cascade Creek. Named for the numerous cascades along its length **(1.7 miles to next point).**

Turnoff to Big Oak Flat Road on north side of road. Big Oak Flat Road leads to the community of Big Oak Flat, the Tuolumne sequoia grove, Crane Flat, and the Tioga Road, which goes to Tuolumne Meadows, and across the Sierra to Lee Vining **(0.9 miles to next point).**

End of this highway stretch. Merced Road joins the Yosemite Valley Loop Road.

INTERESTING NEARBY SITES

Mono Lake National Scenic Area

The seventy-four thousand-acre Mono Lake National Scenic Area was designated by Congress in 1984. The designation acknowledged the outstanding scenic, geological, biological, and historical values of the Mono Lake Basin.

The centerpiece for the Scenic Area is Mono Lake, thirteen miles long by eight miles wide, set at the base of the towering east wall of the Sierra Nevada. This salty sea—a miniature Great Salt Lake—lies within the Great Basin bioregion, a sagebrush-dominated cold desert that stretches from the Sierra to the Wasatch Range in Utah. Streams entering the lake carry trace amounts of salts and other minerals. With no outlet, some lake waters are evaporated, leaving behind concentrated salts, contributing to the lake's briny nature that is two and one-half times as saline as the Pacific Ocean.

Although the lake is too salty for fish, it is home to brine shrimp and brine flies. These invertebrates provide food for numerous bird species that congregate at the lake during migration and the breeding season. As many as 750,000 eared grebes, one-third of the North American population, descend upon Mono Lake during migration to forage for shrimp and refuel for the next leg of their journey. In addition, 60,000 red-necked phalaropes and 90,000 Wilson's phalaropes make Mono Lake a major stopover during migration. Other waterfowl and shorebirds halt at the lake for days or weeks at a time. Mono Lake is home to 90 percent of the California gulls in California. So important is the lake for some species that it was recently included in the Western Hemisphere Shorebird Reserve Network.

Among the attractions of Mono Lake, aside from its wildlife abundance, are the tufa deposits that line its shores. Water from the adjacent

Sierra Nevada flows in underground channels, boiling up as springs beneath the lake surface. This springwater has high levels of calcium, which combines with carbonates in the lake to form tufa, limestone towers and pillars, up to thirty feet in height. As the lake level has dropped, these tufa towers have been exposed, creating castle-like formations. New tufa towers are still being formed beneath the lake's surface.

In addition to the tufa deposits, volcanic eruptions continue to alter the basin's topography. Negit Island erupted 1,700 years ago, and the origin of Paoha Island can be traced to an eruption within the last 330 years. Hot springs and craters are still found on Paoha. Most of the California gulls breeding at Mono Lake use Negit Island for nesting.

Mono Lake, one of the oldest lakes in North America, has occupied this basin for at least seventy thousand years and has been as much as sixty times its present size. Old lake shorelines, recording its higher levels, can be seen against the base of the Sierra. Despite its age, Mono Lake was once on its way to extinction. In 1941 the Los Angeles Department of Water and Power (LADWP), seeking to expand its eastern Sierra water supplies, began to divert the water from Rush Creek, Lee Vining Creek, Parker Creek, and Walker Creek—streams that supplied Mono Lake with much of its water. This diversion took a significant environmental toll. Without the input of additional fresh water, the lake's level has dropped forty feet causing salinity to double and overall volume to drop by half. Dust from the exposed shorelines now pollutes the mountain air. Furthermore, the dewatering of the Mono Lake tributaries destroyed several important trout fisheries and reduced the amount of riparian habitat.

Concerned that the declining water level threatened the brine shrimp and brine flies that support the multitude of bird species, David Gaines, a young ornithologist living in Lee Vining, formed the Mono Lake Committee in 1978. The committee initiated efforts to save the lake. In 1979 the National Audubon Society (NAS) joined the fray and sued the LADWP. NAS lawyers argued under the public trust doctrine that the city's use of the Mono Basin waters could not occur at the expense of the lake's ecosystem. In 1983 the California Supreme Court ruled in favor of the Audubon Society. In 1989 the state of California established a $60 million fund to protect Mono Lake, and in 1990 the courts ordered Los Angeles to restore the streams it had been dewatering to ensure a minimum lake level that would protect Mono Lake's unique qualities. Despite these changes, the lake's level has continued to drop, prompting the U.S.

Fish and Wildlife Service to propose listing the lake's brine shrimp as a threatened species.

To get acquainted with Mono Lake, a stop at the Inyo National Forest visitor center, overlooking the lake by Lee Vining, is worth the time. A good place to visit the lakeshore is at the South Tufa area, where a nature trail describes the lake's ecological and geological attributes. The tufa area is located 4.5 miles east of Highway 395 off of Highway 120.

Bodie Ghost Town

Lying northeast of Mono Lake is Bodie, a restored ghost town. Bodie was established in 1877 when gold was discovered in the dry, sagebrush hills that lie east of the Sierra near the Nevada border. At its peak, more than ten thousand people called Bodie home. Between 1877 and 1888, miners took $35 million in silver and gold from Bodie mines. After the mines played out in the 1880s, most of the townspeople moved on. Cyanide leach processing brought about a resurgence of the town's population around the turn of the century; this too was shortlived, and by the 1940s the town was abandoned.

During Bodie's heyday, wood to construct and heat homes came from the Jeffrey pine forests to the south of Mono Lake. Some estimate that Bodie residents required more than forty-five thousand cords of wood a year. To move the wood to the town, a railway was built that circled the eastern shore of Mono Lake. The railway has since been torn up, although the general route can still be discerned.

Today the buildings are in a state of "arrested decay" and Bodie, the largest preserved ghost town in the West, is protected within Bodie State Historical Park. The park has no camping facilities, stores, or restaurants, and is open only between 9:00 A.M. and 7:00 P.M. daily. Bodie is reached by a well-maintained dirt road off of Highway 395 between Bridgeport and Lee Vining.

Devil's Postpile National Monument

Located east of Mammoth Lakes along the Middle Fork of the San Joaquin River, the Devil's Postpile National Monument preserves a spectacular lava formation. The land around the Postpile was once part of the original 1891 boundaries of Yosemite National Park, but was deleted from the park, along with other areas, in 1905 as a result of pressure from miners.

The eight-hundred-acre monument was established in 1911 by presidential proclamation to protect it from miners who wanted to dynamite the formation to create a rock dam across the San Joaquin River.

The Postpile, an outcrop of six-sided columnar basalt, was created one million years ago when a molten river of lava four hundred feet thick flowed down the valley. As the basalt cooled, it shrank and cracked, creating the columnar "posts" we see today. Finishing touches were added some forty thousand years ago when glaciers scoured away the tops of the pile, leaving a smooth, glacially polished surface that looks something like a tile floor.

Just north lie the Soda Springs, highly carbonized mineral springs. Also in the monument are Rainbow Falls, where water cascades over an andesite cliff.

Mammoth-Mono Volcanos

Stretching in a thirty-mile-long northeast-southwest line from Mammoth Mountain to Mono Lake is one of the youngest and most active volcanic fields in the United States. Most of the activity has been centered on a ten-mile-long fault where magma from deep in the earth reaches the surface. Eruptions have occurred as recently as the 1800s, and more than twenty eruptions have occurred in the last two thousand years. Earthquakes continue to rattle the area, demonstrating that future eruptions are probable.

A number of volcanic sites can be seen along Highway 395 between Mammoth Lakes and Lee Vining. Just south of Mono Lake are the Mono Craters. Rising twenty-four hundred feet above the valley, the craters are actually volcanic domes. Built of viscous lava, these domes rose slowly like thick toothpaste, creating a plug that blocked further lava flow. The most recent eruption occurred within the last six hundred years. Negit and Paoha Islands in Mono Lake are the northern extensions of this same volcanic group.

Pumice blown free while the craters were formed lies as thick as twenty feet to the east of the domes. The pumice here is mined; this is the only such commercial operation in the United States.

Obsidian, a volcanic glass formed when lava cools rapidly, is the same chemical composition as pumice, but its process of formation is different. Pumice is created when magma is exploded from a volcano, filling the molten rock with air. Obsidian is oozed from the surface and solidifies quickly. Indians used obsidian to make arrowheads, and flakes of this rock were one of the major trade items carried across the Sierra. Obsidian Dome, a three-hundred-foot-high hill that lies 1.5 miles off Highway 395 north of Mammoth Lakes, can be reached by an easy hike.

The Inyo Craters are two small pits created by volcanic eruption approximately six hundred years ago. These craters were formed when groundwater came in contact with magma, became superheated, and exploded. The craters are located off the Mammoth Lakes Scenic Loop road.

Occupying a portion of the Long Valley caldera, the Hot Creek geological site is marked by clouds of steam. Showing up in thermal springs, fumaroles (gas vents), and even geyser eruptions, the hot water is created when groundwater comes in contact with magma five to eight miles under the earth's surface. Water in this system takes up to a thousand years to circulate.

Wilderness Areas

Surrounding Yosemite National Park are lands administered by the National Forest Service. Although activities prohibited within national parks such as off-road-vehicle travel, logging, mining, and livestock grazing occur on many Forest Service lands, some areas have been designated wilderness, which precludes all of these activities except livestock grazing (an obvious oversight in the law that greatly compromises the value of wilderness designation) and mandates preservation of wildlands and ecological integrity. Wilderness designation does permit recreational activities such as hiking, camping, fishing, hunting, and skiing. It serves to protect watersheds and wildlife habitat. Because so much of the surrounding Forest Service lands are designated wilderness, Yosemite is part of a large roadless complex that stretches nearly two hundred miles from Sonora Pass in the north to Walker Pass in the south, with the only break occurring at Tioga Pass. The following wilderness areas flank Yosemite's borders.

Ansel Adams Wilderness

The Ansel Adams Wilderness, formerly the Minarets Wilderness, was enlarged and renamed by the 1984 California Wilderness Act. This lake-studded wilderness borders Yosemite National Park on the east and south, taking in much of the area that was removed from Yosemite's borders by the 1905 deletions. Today the wilderness straddles the Sierra Nevada, covering portions of both the Sierra and Inyo national forests.

The area encompasses the North, Middle, and a portion of the South Fork of the San Joaquin River. Elevations vary between 7,000 and nearly 14,000 feet. Although forests of lodgepole pine, red fir, Jeffrey pine, and aspen occur, much of the area is barren granite. Both the John Muir and Pacific Crest trails cross the wilderness. The Minarets—stark, jagged, volcanic peaks—form a sawtoothed backbone along the headwaters of the San Joaquin.

Hoover Wilderness

Lying north and east of Yosemite National Park is the 48,622-acre Hoover Wilderness. The Hoover is studded with lakes and meadows, plus small aspen groves at lower elevations. Mining occurred until the 1950s. Tailings from the Hess Tungsten Mine are still visible by Steelhead Lake, and old miners' cabins are scattered in other portions of the wilderness farther north. Just north and west of the Hoover is the West Fork of the Walker River, presently outside the designated wilderness. It is one of the largest remaining roadless lands and potential wilderness additions in the entire Sierra Nevada.

Emigrant Wilderness

The northern boundary of Yosemite on the western slope of the Sierra is shared with the 117,596-acre Emigrant Wilderness. Looking much like Yosemite's backcountry, the wilderness is characterized by rounded granite domes interspersed with more than one hundred lakes, meadows and forests of aspen and lodgepole pine, and numerous peaks capped with volcanic rocks. The wilderness takes its name from the emigrants drawn to California's goldfields who crossed this portion of the Sierra in the 1850s.

Jeffrey Pine Forest

The world's largest pure stand of Jeffrey pine lies in a belt east and north of Mammoth Lakes. Jeffrey pine is similar in appearance to ponderosa pine but tends to have larger cones and bright red bark. The abundance of Jeffrey pine is the result of a gap in the Sierra Nevada to the west. Low saddles along the Middle Fork of the San Joaquin permit winter storms, normally blocked by the high Sierra, to cross the mountains, allowing additional water to reach this portion of the eastern Sierra. The forest exists in what would otherwise be a sagebrush desert.

Merced Wild and Scenic River

The Merced River begins at 11,000 feet in Yosemite National Park and flows west to join the San Joaquin River. A total of 122 miles of the river are protected from dam construction because of its designation as a wild and scenic river. The respective sections of the river corridor are administered by the Bureau of Land Management and Forest Service. The river is divided into three designations: seventy-nine "wild" miles, fourteen "scenic" miles, and twenty-nine "recreational" miles (followed by a road).

The twenty-eight-mile stretch of the Merced between Red Bud and Bagby are floated during the high-water season of April and June. There are a number of Class IV rapids. An old railroad right-of-way provides a twenty-eight-mile level trail that can be hiked along the lower canyon.

Tuolumne Wild and Scenic River

The Tuolumne is the other major river that flows from Yosemite National Park. Some eighty-three miles of the Tuolumne are protected as wild and scenic river with forty-seven miles designated as "wild," twenty-three miles as "scenic," and thirteen miles as "recreational." Both the National Park Service and Stanislaus National Forest manage the river corridor that begins below Hetch Hetchy Reservoir. Rafters run the river between May and October.

Nelder Sequoia Grove

Sequoia groves are a rare feature in the Sierra Nevada. Only seventy-five groves are scattered along a two-hundred-mile belt that flanks the western slope of the range. In addition to the three groves of giant sequoias within Yosemite National Park, another grove, the Nelder, lies in the Sierra National Forest south of Highway 41 between Oak Hurst and Yosemite's southern entrance. A one-mile, self-guided "Shadow of the Giants" trail winds through giant sequoias mixed with large sugar pines, incense cedars, and white firs.

BIRD LIST

The following species can be expected to be seen sometime, somewhere in Yosemite. Some species are migratory; others breed in the park. Some may be abundant only in summer. Others, like the bald eagle, are always rare, but more common in winter, spring, and fall. The abundance of each species is rated by the number system listed below. The higher the number, the more common the species. Keep in mind the fact that some species, such as peregrine falcon, are relatively uncommon, yet they may be common in Yosemite in relation to their overall numbers or distribution.

Common to abundant (4)
Uncommon (3)
Rare (2)
Very rare (1)

Herons

____ Great blue heron (2)

Grebes

____ Eared grebe (2)

Ducks

____ Mallard (2)
____ Harlequin duck (1)
____ Common merganser (1)

Hawks

____ Turkey vulture (1)
____ Bald eagle (1)
____ Northern harrier (1)
____ Red-tailed hawk (3)
____ Golden eagle (2)
____ American kestrel (3)

Hawks (continued)

_____ Sharp-shinned hawk (2)   _____ Peregrine falcon (2)
_____ Cooper's hawk (2)   _____ Prairie falcon (2)
_____ Northern hawk (2)

Grouse

_____ Blue grouse (3)   _____ White-tailed ptarmigan (2)

Quail

_____ Mountain quail (4)

Water Birds

_____ Killdeer (2)   _____ California gull (3)
_____ Spotted sandpiper (3)

Doves

_____ Band-tailed pigeon (3)   _____ Mourning dove (2)

Owls

_____ Flammulated owl (3)   _____ Spotted owl (2)
_____ Western screech owl (1)   _____ Great gray owl (2)
_____ Great horned owl (3)   _____ Long-eared owl (1)
_____ Northern pygmy owl (3)   _____ Northern saw-whet owl (2)

Nighthawks

_____ Common nighthawk (2)   _____ Poorwill (2)

Swifts

_____ Black swift (4)   _____ White-throated swift (4)
_____ Vaux's swift (1)

Hummingbirds

_____ Black-chinned humming-   _____ Calliope hummingbird (3)
bird (1)   _____ Rufous hummingbird (4)
_____ Anna's hummingbird (2)   _____ Belted kingfisher (2)

Woodpeckers

_____ Lewis' woodpecker (1)   _____ Downy woodpecker (3)

Woodpeckers *(continued)*

____ Acorn woodpecker (4)

____ Red-naped sapsucker (2)

____ Red-breasted sapsucker (3)

____ Williamson's sapsucker (3)

____ Nuttall's woodpecker (2)

____ Pileated woodpecker (2)

____ Hairy woodpecker (3)

____ White-headed woodpecker (3)

____ Black-backed woodpecker (2)

____ Northern flicker (4)

Flycatchers

____ Olive-sided flycatcher (4)

____ Western wood pewee (4)

____ Willow flycatcher (2)

____ Hammond's flycatcher (4)

____ Dusky flycatcher (4)

____ Western flycatcher (2)

____ Black phoebe (2)

____ Say's phoebe (1)

____ Ash-throated flycatcher (1)

____ Western kingbird (1)

Larks

____ Horned lark (2)

Swallows

____ Tree swallows (2)

____ Violet-green swallow (4)

____ Northern rough-winged swallow (3)

____ Cliff swallow (2)

____ Barn swallow (3)

Jays

____ Steller's jay (4)

____ Shrub jay (2)

____ Pinyon jay (1)

____ Clark's nutcracker (4)

____ American crow (1)

____ Common raven (3)

Chickadees, Creepers, Titmice, and Nuthatches

____ Mountain chickadee (4)

____ Chestnut-backed chickadee (2)

____ Plain titmouse (2)

____ Bushtit (3)

____ Red-breasted nuthatch (4)

____ White-breasted nuthatch (3)

____ Pygmy nuthatch (1)

____ Brown creeper (4)

Wrens

____ Rock wren (3)

____ House wren (3)

Wrens *(continued)*

____ Canyon wren (3)   ____ Winter wren (2)
____ Bewick's wren (1)

Dipper

____ American dipper (4)

Kinglets

____ Golden-crowned kinglet (4)   ____ Blue-gray gnatcatcher (2)
____ Ruby-crowned kinglet (3)

Thrushes

____ Western bluebird (2)   ____ American robin (4)
____ Mountain bluebird (3)   ____ Varied thrush (3)
____ Townsend's solitaire (3)   ____ Wrentit (3)
____ Hermit thrush (4)

Pipits

____ Water pipit (1)

Waxwings

____ Cedar waxwing (2)

Shrikes

____ Loggerhead shrike (2)

Starling

____ European starling (3)

Vireos

____ Solitary vireo (4)   ____ Warbling vireo (4)
____ Hutton's vireo (2)

Warblers

____ Oranged-crowned warbler (4)   ____ Townsend's warbler (2)
____ Nashville warbler (4)   ____ Hermit warbler (4)
____ Yellow warbler (4)   ____ MacGillivray's warbler (4)
____ Yellow-rumped warbler (4)   ____ Common yellowthroat (1)

Warblers *(continued)*

_____ Black-throated gray warbler (4)

_____ Wilson's warbler (2)

Tanagers

_____ Western tanager (4)

Grosbeak

_____ Black-headed grosbeak (4)

Buntings

_____ Lazuli bunting (2)

Sparrows and Juncos

_____ Green-tailed towhee (2)

_____ Rufous-sided towhee (3)

_____ Brown towhee (2)

_____ Chipping sparrow (4)

_____ Fox sparrow (4)

_____ Song sparrow (4)

_____ Lincoln's sparrow (4)

_____ Golden-crowned sparrow (2)

_____ White-crowned sparrow (4)

_____ Dark-eyed junco (4)

Orioles and Blackbirds

_____ Red-winged blackbird (3)

_____ Western meadowlark (1)

_____ Brewer's blackbird (4)

_____ Brown-headed cowbird (4)

_____ Northern oriole (3)

Finches

_____ Rosy finch (4)

_____ Pine grosbeak (4)

_____ Cassin finch (4)

_____ Red crossbill (3)

_____ Pine siskin (4)

_____ Lesser goldfinch (3)

_____ Lawrence's goldfinch (2)

_____ Evening grosbeak (4)

MAMMAL LIST

Opossums

_____ Opossum

Shrews

_____ Mount Lyell shrew   _____ Ornate shrew
_____ Vagrant shrew   _____ Water shrew
_____ Dusky shrew   _____ Trowbridge's shrew

Moles

_____ Broad-footed mole

Bats

_____ Little brown myotis   _____ Western pipistrelle
_____ Yuma myotis   _____ Big brown bat
_____ Long-eared myotis   _____ Red bat
_____ Fringed myotis   _____ Hoary bat
_____ Long-legged myotis   _____ Spotted bat
_____ California myotis   _____ Townsend's big-eared bat
_____ Small-footed myotis   _____ Pallid bat
_____ Silver-haired bat   _____ Brazilian free-tailed bat

Pikas, Rabbits, and Hares

_____ Pika   _____ Snowshoe hare
_____ Brush rabbit   _____ White-tailed jackrabbit
_____ Desert cottontail   _____ Black-tailed jackrabbit

Mountain Beavers

_____ Mountain beaver

Chipmunks

_____ Alpine chipmunks   _____ Merriam's chipmunk
_____ Yellow pine chipmunk   _____ Long-eared chipmunk
_____ Allen's chipmunk   _____ Lodgepole chipmunk

Marmots, Ground Squirrels, and Tree Squirrels

_____ Yellow-bellied marmot   _____ Western gray squirrel
_____ Belding's ground squirrel   _____ Douglas squirrel
_____ California ground squirrel   _____ Northern flying squirrel
_____ Golden-mantled ground
      squirrel

Pocket Gophers

_____ Botta's pocket gopher   _____ Mountain pocket gopher

Pocket Mice

_____ California pocket mouse

Kangaroo Rats

_____ Heermann's kangaroo rat

Mice

_____ Western harvest mouse   _____ Pinyon mouse
_____ Deer mouse   _____ Western jumping mouse
_____ Brush mouse

Wood Rats

_____ Dusky-footed wood rat   _____ Brushy-tailed wood rat

Voles

_____ Heather vole   _____ California vole
_____ Montane vole   _____ Long-tailed vole

Porcupines

_____ Porcupine

Canids

_____ Coyote   _____ Gray fox
_____ Red fox

Bears

_____ Black bear

Raccoon Family

_____ Ringtail   _____ Raccoon

Weasel Family

_____ Marten   _____ Wolverine
_____ Fisher   _____ Badger
_____ Ermine   _____ Western spotted skunk
_____ Long-tailed weasel   _____ Striped skunk
_____ Mink   _____ River otter

Cat Family

_____ Mountain lion   _____ Bobcat

Deer

_____ Mule deer

Bighorns

_____ Bighorn sheep

THREATENED, ENDANGERED, AND SENSITIVE SPECIES

The following animals and plants are considered threatened, endangered, or sensitive species, and were known or suspected to have been found in Yosemite National Park as of December 1991.

Listed Species

Birds

Bald eagle
Peregrine falcon

Fishes

Paiute cutthroat trout
(not native to Yosemite)

Candidates for Listing

Amphibians

California red-legged frog
Foothill yellow-legged frog
Mountain yellow-legged frog
Limestone salamander
Mount Lyell salamander
Yosemite toad

Birds

Northern goshawk
California horned lark
California spotted owl
Loggerhead shrike
Mountain quail

Mammals

Spotted bat
Greater western mastiff bat
Pacific fisher
Sierra Nevada red fox
Sierra Nevada snowshoe hare
California bighorn sheep
Mount Lyell shrew
California wolverine

Reptiles

Giant garter snake
    (same as western aquatic garter snake)

Invertebrates

Wawona riffle beetle
Bohart's blue butterfly
Mono checkerspot butterfly
Sierra pygmy grasshopper
Merced Canyon shoulderband
Indian Yosemite snail

Plants

Bolander's clover
Yosemite woolly sunflower
Hetch Hetchy monkeyflower

FIELD GUIDE TO PLANTS AND ANIMALS

Indian paintbrush

western columbine

lupine

alder leaves and catkins   red-osier dogwood   black cottonwood

wood rose   serviceberry   shrubby cinquefoil

Douglas-fir   thimbleberry

aspen leaves and catkins   lodgepole pine   whitebark pine

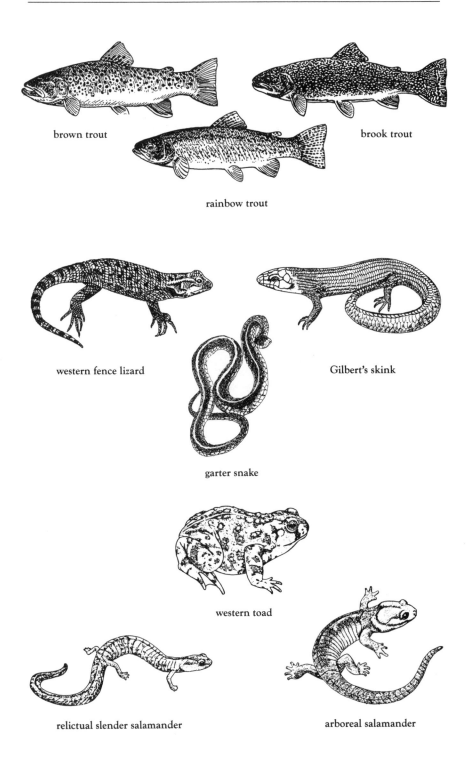

brown trout

brook trout

rainbow trout

western fence lizard

Gilbert's skink

garter snake

western toad

relictual slender salamander

arboreal salamander

long-toed salamander   limestone salamander

California newt

western pond turtle   mountain yellow-legged frog   Pacific tree frog

northern flicker   sharp-shinned hawk   barn swallow

white-breasted nuthatch   house wren   plain titmouse

great horned owl   golden eagle   American kestrel

red-tailed hawk   belted kingfisher   violet-green swallow

water ouzel   common nighthawk   Clark's nutcracker

American robin   yellow-rumped warbler   red-winged blackbird

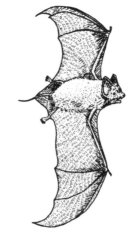

dark-eyed junco   Brazilian free-tailed bat   dusky-footed wood rat

western harvest mouse   western jumping mouse   long-tailed mole

heather vole   mountain pocket gopher   Heerman's kangaroo rat

long-eared chipmunk   Belding's ground squirrel   flying squirrel

Douglas squirrel

snowshoe hare

white-tailed jack rabbit

mink

marten

short-tailed weasel

badger

striped skunk

river otter

ringtail raccoon   fisher   raccoon

mountain lion   bobcat   fox

black bear   mule deer   bighorn sheep

INDEX